Especially For

....

From

....

Date

....

Come Away
My Beloved

A Daily Devotional

Frances J. Roberts

Come Away
My Beloved

A Daily Devotional

SHILOH RUN PRESS
An Imprint of Barbour Publishing, Inc.

Compiled by Pamela L. McQuade from the books *Come Away My Beloved* © 1970, *Progress of Another Pilgrim* © 1970, *Dialogues with God* © 1968, *On the Highroad of Surrender* © 1973, and *Make Haste My Beloved* © 1978.

Print ISBN 978-1-68322-482-2

eBook Editions:
Adobe Digital Edition (.epub) 978-1-68322-663-5
Kindle and MobiPocket Edition (.prc) 978-1-68322-664-2

All scripture quotations, unless otherwise noted, are taken from the King James Version of the Bible.

Scripture quotations marked NKJV are taken from the New King James Version®. Copyright © 1982 by Thomas Nelson, Inc. Used by permission. All rights reserved.

Published by Shiloh Run Press, an imprint of Barbour Publishing, Inc., P.O. Box 719, Uhrichsville, Ohio 44683, www.shilohrunpress.com

Our mission is to inspire the world with the life-changing message of the Bible.

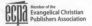

Member of the
Evangelical Christian
Publishers Association

Printed in China.

Introduction

"Forged in the crucible of life" is how author Frances J. Roberts describes her million-selling book *Come Away My Beloved*, selections of which you'll find throughout this devotional. Excerpts from her other books—*Progress of Another Pilgrim, Dialogues with God, On the Highroad of Surrender*, and *Make Haste My Beloved*—are also included in this first-ever, 365-day compilation of Mrs. Roberts's writings.

The preface to *Come Away My Beloved* applies equally to all of Frances Roberts's works:

> *In the midst of each day's joys and trials has come the ministering Spirit of the Heavenly Father and the Lord Jesus Christ, bringing words of encouragement, hope, comfort, and conviction.*

To gain the maximum blessing from this book, read it carefully and prayerfully, a little at a time, searching always for the special treasure of truth for your own need. He who knows you by name and understands your deepest longings will speak to your heart from these pages, shutting out the world around you and bringing you into fellowship with Himself.

Whether you are just beginning your Christian walk or have grown into a fuller stature in Christ, you will be equally challenged and helped. Some books give instruction for Christian living; others inspire to greater devotion. This book will do both as you open your soul to its living message.

With this book go many prayers that God will enrich every

life it touches. Surely we are all bound together in one family in Christ through the bonds of His Holy Spirit.

Each day for an entire year, you'll find a thought-provoking excerpt from one of Frances J. Roberts's books, a relevant scripture, and a question prompting further reflection. Our hope is that, for the next year, the *Come Away My Beloved Daily Devotional* will draw you ever more closely to the Father's heart.

The Master Artist

from *Come Away My Beloved*

And God saw every thing that he had made,
and, behold, it was very good.

GENESIS 1:31

———◦┼◦———◦┼◦———◦┼◦———

I make no idle strokes. What I do is never haphazard. I am never merely mixing colors out of casual curiosity. My every move is one of vital creativity, and every stroke is part of the whole.

Never be dismayed by apparent incongruity. Never be alarmed by a sudden dash of color seemingly out of context. Say only to your questioning heart, "It is the Infinite wielding His brush; I know He does all things well."

What good thing might God be creating in my life right now?

Prepare!

from *Make Haste My Beloved*

And God said unto Noah. . . .
Make thee an ark of gopher wood.

GENESIS 6:13-14

---

*Y*our own future is shaped by today's decisions; therefore, the future should not be ignored as though irrelevant to today. Jesus did not teach man to ignore the future, but to prepare for it. His warning was against anxiety concerning tomorrow, not against preparation.

It was I who taught Noah to prepare for the flood. Draw on My wisdom, for to Me all things are plain now.

What preparations should I be making in my life now?

There Is Always an Alternative

from *Progress of Another Pilgrim*

And he said, Take now thy son, thine only son Isaac,
whom thou lovest, and get thee into the land of Moriah;
and offer him there for a burnt offering upon one
of the mountains which I will tell thee of.

GENESIS 22:2

*N*o price is too great to pay for the proper care of that which I have given you. Never regard lightly that which is precious in My sight. There is always an alternative to the life of relinquishment, but it is lean and barren. That which is most precious needs to be offered up to Me continually.

My grace is as a beacon. It shall shed light on all that is now obscure.

What precious thing do I need to offer up to God?

Relinquish Your Will

from *Come Away My Beloved*

And God sent me before you to preserve
you a posterity in the earth, and to save
your lives by a great deliverance.

GENESIS 45:7

*M*y heart is grieved by your independence. How would Joseph have felt if his father and family had remained at home, starving in the famine, when he had invited them to share the bountiful stores he had at his disposal and desired to share freely with them?

Would he not have grieved far more deeply than over the unjust actions of his brothers who hated him? For to be rebuffed by a loved one causes pain not to be compared with the cruelties inflicted by an enemy.

In what areas do I need to relinquish my will to God?

Release Others

from *Progress of Another Pilgrim*

But as for you, ye thought evil against me;
but God meant it unto good, to bring to pass,
as it is this day, to save much people alive.

GENESIS 50:20

I do not need to remove the difficulty. It is no real problem to Me. It is only an anxiety manifesting itself in your mind and claiming the power to destroy.

I am restricted when you hold negative thoughts about the actions of other people. Release them to Me; otherwise, you turn the action upon yourself to your own hurt.

*What negative thoughts might I be
holding toward other people's actions?*

Household Salvation

from *Come Away My Beloved*

For the LORD will pass through to smite the Egyptians;
and when he seeth the blood upon the lintel, and on the two
side posts, the LORD will pass over the door, and will not suffer
the destroyer to come in unto your houses to smite you.

EXODUS 12:23

I have blessed you out of the bounties of heaven and have
not withheld from you what your heart has desired. Yes, and I
would do still more. For have I not promised that you and your
household should be saved? Wasn't the blood applied to the
lintel and the doorposts for the salvation of the entire family?
So renew your energies, and know that I am working with you.

*What family member or friend might need
my prayers for salvation today?*

The Fear of God

from *Make Haste My Beloved*

Thou shalt have no other gods before me.

EXODUS 20:3

*Y*es, My child, if you would search Me out, learn what it is to know the fear of God. Make of your heart a citadel of sacred worship, knowing that as you kneel at the altar of consecration, you shall receive of My grace and mercy and you shall behold mysteries. . .things hidden from the carnal eye and withheld from the self-absorbed. For love of self will keep you from this place as surely as baser sins.

How can I make my heart a "citadel of sacred worship"?

The Kingdom of Lights

from *Make Haste My Beloved*

And he said, I beseech thee,
shew me thy glory.

EXODUS 33:18

---

*D*o not fear darkness: fear God, and He shall be to you a light. The world is enshrouded in darkness, but they who walk in My truth walk in light. My kingdom is a kingdom of light, and clear, purified vessels are the transmitters of My glory in the darkened world. *Shine,* My children, and darkness shall be scattered as you walk!

How can I shine God's light into a dark world today?

This Is the Glory Life

from *Dialogues with God*

For the cloud of the LORD was upon the tabernacle by day,
and fire was on it by night, in the sight of all the house
of Israel, throughout all their journeys.

EXODUS 40:38

*B*ehold, I say unto thee, *This is the way, walk ye in it,* neither turn to the right hand nor to the left.

For I shall make the path for thy feet a plain path, and light shall be there, and there shall be the shining of My glory.

It shall not be the glory of man. It shall be the glory of God.

How has God smoothed and lit my path through life?

The Oil of Consecration

from *Progress of Another Pilgrim*

In a pan it shall be made with oil; and when it is baken,
thou shalt bring it in: and the baken pieces of the meat
offering shalt thou offer for a sweet savour unto the LORD.
And the priest of his sons that is anointed in his stead
shall offer it: it is a statute for ever unto the LORD;
it shall be wholly burnt.

LEVITICUS 6:21-22

All your ministry must be blessed by the oil of consecration. Not one thing can be withheld. That which is most precious must be daily offered in dedication. Anything which is unworthy or evil must be given to Me so that it may be taken away; but the pure and good must be given to Me also, so that you may be continually freed from clasping it to yourself.

Anything you grasp becomes a burden. Give all to Me in a daily morning offering.

What am I grasping that I should be giving to God today?

Obedience, the Fabric of Happiness

from *Make Haste My Beloved*

Ye shall do my judgments, and keep mine ordinances,
to walk therein: I am the LORD your God.

LEVITICUS 18:4

*L*ook to Me, My child, and all your needs will be met by My abundant provision. I will not suffer the enemy to overthrow him who puts his confidence in Me. I am faithful to My Word, and I have promised never to fail nor to forsake.

Obedience is the fabric of happiness. To rebel is to seek sorrow. Only a yielded heart can find rest in Me, and to know contentment there must be resignation of personal rights in favor of My will.

In what areas do I need to yield my heart to God?

Hold Your Ground

from *On the Highroad of Surrender*

Let us go up at once, and posess it;
for we are well able to overcome it.

NUMBERS 13:30

I have not brought you out of the wilderness to allow you to be devoured by the giants in the land. I brought you out by a miracle of My divine grace, and I bring you in that you may experience My delivering power as you are confronted by the enemy in all his varied strategy and devices.

Stretch forth the hand of faith. Set foot upon the territory you wish to claim. I will move ahead of you and clear a path, but you must be determined to follow closely and to hold your ground without wavering.

What territory do I wish to claim, through faith in God?

Outer Blessing and Inner Strength

from *On the Highroad of Surrender*

But My servant Caleb, because he has a different spirit in him
and has followed Me fully, I will bring into the land where he
went, and his descendants shall inherit it.

NUMBERS 14:24 NKJV

Ponder for a moment what great crises would face you if
tomorrow all your prayers were answered! Could you bear it?
The new joy. . .the added responsibility? Therefore, when you
pray, ask not only for the desired results, but also that your
heart will be strengthened to receive, and that added wisdom
be given to meet the new problems.

You have watched some succeed only to fail. This occurs
when outer blessings are sought and inner strength neglected.

What new challenges might my answered prayers bring?

Whatsoever You Sow

from *Come Away My Beloved*

Be sure your sin will find you out.

NUMBERS 32:23

*H*ow can I give you healing for your body while there is anxiety in your mind? So long as there is disease in your thoughts, there will be disease in your body. One thing in particular you must develop for your own preservation, and that is an absolute confidence in My loving care.

Only when your mind is at rest can your body build health. Worry is an actively destructive force. Anxiety produces tension, and tension is the road to pain. Fear is devastating to the physical well-being of the body. Anger throws poison into the system that no antibiotic can ever counteract.

"Be sure your sin will find you out," the Bible states (Numbers 32:23). One of the most common ways that hidden sin is revealed is through the maladies of the body.

Where might my soul need healing?

My Holy Spirit Judges

from *Come Away My Beloved*

But if ye will not do so, behold, ye have sinned against
the Lord: and be sure your sin will find you out.

NUMBERS 32:23

*I*f you walk now in the light of My revealed truth and if
you judge yourselves, you will not be judged at that coming
day. And if you allow the searching eye of the Holy Spirit to
find you out, then it will not be said to you, "Your sin will find
you out." Do not resist Me or harden your hearts. Do not pro-
voke Me to use My chastening rod, for I love you.

In what ways have I resisted God's Holy Spirit
in "finding out" my sin?

Give Me the Firstfruits

from *Dialogues with God*

Keep the sabbath day to sanctify it,
as the Lord thy God hath commanded thee.

DEUTERONOMY 5:12

---

*G*ive Me a heart that has learned how to become quiet and to rest. Anybody can work. Few people know how to be quiet. Ye *must* be able to collect yourself—to take time to absorb the Spirit of God. For to be freshly filled with the Spirit will bring the guidance and direction and wisdom *and the will* to do His bidding.

In what ways should I quiet my heart and rest?

The Burden-Bearer

from *Come Away My Beloved*

He might prove thee, to do thee
good at thy latter end.
DEUTERONOMY 8:16

*M*y child, do not share your burdens with all who come to you professing concern. I, Myself, am the great burden-bearer. You need not look to another. I will lead you and guide you in wisdom from above. All things will be as I plan them, if you allow Me the freedom to shape circumstances and lead you to the right decisions.

What burdens should I hand over to God today?

Spiritual Liberty

from *On the Highroad of Surrender*

Arise, go over this Jordan, thou, and all this people,
unto the land which I do give to them,
even to the children of Israel.

JOSHUA 1:2

*A*n entire generation perished in the wilderness because of indecision, for though they were bodily freed, they never wakened to their spiritual liberty; they grieved the spirit of God for forty years and died in the wilderness, never having received the promise (Hebrews 3:15-19).

Bringing you out, My children, is only the beginning. I am bringing sons to glory, and I am preparing a people who shall go in. They shall possess the land. They shall be strong in the Lord, and they shall fulfill My purposes (Joshua 1).

What purposes might God want to fulfill in me?

A Spirit of Gratitude

from *Progress of Another Pilgrim*

Every place that the sole of your foot shall tread upon,
that have I given unto you, as I said unto Moses.

JOSHUA 1:3

My little one, the path has been prepared before you, and you shall not fear, neither hesitate. As you tread, you will find the victory has already been won. No challenge shall turn you aside, no past defeat shall dim your faith in My provision and grace.

Love Me with your whole heart. I am the Lord, your God. I have saved you and healed you, and you have much for which to praise Me. Never stop. The highest occupation of the soul is that of worship and adoration. Never cease to keep a spirit of overflowing gratitude. It shall both sweeten your own spirit and lift your whole ministry into the highest plane.

Have I forgotten to thank God for anything?

He Has Filled My Cup

from *Come Away My Beloved*

And he said, Nay; but as captain of the host of the
Lord am I now come. And Joshua fell on his face
to the earth, and did worship, and said unto him,
What saith my Lord unto his servant?

JOSHUA 5:14

I stand before you as the Mighty Captain of the Hosts of
the Almighty, And you as men of war. (See Joshua 5:13-15.) We
seek no longer
 To rest in green pastures and lie beside still waters; For I
have issued my command to wipe out the giants, And to utterly
destroy the inhabitants of the land.

What commands does the Mighty Captain have for my life?

Fear, a Sin

from *On the Highroad of Surrender*

Hebron therefore became the inheritance of Caleb
the son of Jephunneh the Kenezite unto this day,
because that he wholly followed the LORD God of Israel.

JOSHUA 14:14

*B*e not faint of heart. Fear will rob you of your possession
as quickly as any other sin; for truly fear is a sin and it opens
the door for many other sins to follow.

Guard your heart from doubt and every negative attitude.
You cannot afford to take the risk of entertaining any such
thoughts at so critical a time. Only the strong in faith shall
prevail. Only those with a "Caleb" spirit shall take the walled
cities and crush out the enemies.

Is mine a "Caleb" spirit?

Prepare!

from *Make Haste My Beloved*

And the LORD said unto Gideon, By the three hundred
men that lapped will I save you, and deliver
the Midianites into thine hand: and let all the
other people go every man unto his place.

JUDGES 7:7

*I*t was I who taught Noah to prepare for the flood (Genesis 6:13-22). I gave Joseph wisdom as to how to prepare for the seven-year famine (Genesis 41). I showed Gideon how to prepare his army in advance of the battle (Judges 7). The message of John the Baptist was a message of preparation: "Prepare ye the way of the LORD" (Isaiah 40:3). I have taught you to be prepared for the second coming (Matthew 24:44).

Yes, the riches of the future are for those who make preparation today. Draw on My wisdom, for to Me all things are plain now.

What wisdom do I need from God to prepare for my future?

You Shall Not Be Earthbound

from *Come Away My Beloved*

And Ruth said. . . .whither thou goest, I will go;
and where thou lodgest, I will lodge:
thy people shall be my people, and thy God my God.

RUTH 1:16

*R*eceive My love freely. Drink of My Spirit. And mount up on the wings of My power. For there are powers of the air to be subdued and conquered. You need faith and the liberty and power of the Holy Spirit to overcome these and rise above them.

My Church shall be an overcoming church, and My Bride shall be a heavenly being. I will not choose a wife out of Egypt. I will take to Me one who has chosen to make My home her home and My people her people, even as Ruth did. But she who turns back, like Orpah, shall not enter into My inheritance.

Am I a Ruth or an Orpah?

Find Solitude

from *Come Away My Beloved*

O Lord of hosts, if thou wilt indeed look on the affliction of
thine handmaid, and remember me, and not forget thine
handmaid, but wilt give unto thine handmaid a man child,
then I will give him unto the Lord all the days of his life,
and there shall no razor come upon his head.

1 SAMUEL 1:11

There is no blessing I would withhold from those who walk
in obedience to Me. Near to My heart and precious in My sight
are those who have eyes to discern My purpose and ears that
listen to My direction.

Do not be intent on great accomplishments. By what
standards do you judge the importance of a matter? It was a
relatively small thing that Hannah prayed for a son, but what
great things I accomplished through Samuel!

What small things can I offer up to God today?

Faith and the Delivering Angel

from *Progress of Another Pilgrim*

Thy servant slew both the lion and the bear:
and this uncircumcised Philistine shall be as one of them,
seeing he hath defied the armies of the living God.

1 SAMUEL 17:36

I slew the lion and the bear," said David, and having thus developed courage, he moved unflinchingly to confront the giant Philistine. That which had been tried in solitude broke into evidence in the public crisis. It was in this area of faith and courage that he was above his fellows.

Secret faith had its moment of open revelation. It is ever so. Build inner faith from the lesser challenges, and it will be your delivering angel in the most calamitous moment.

Am I building inner faith?

Recognize My Hand

from *Progress of Another Pilgrim*

He brought me forth also into a large place:
he delivered me, because he delighted in me.

2 SAMUEL 22:20

I have assured you that there would be a reward for your faithfulness. You are now at a place where you can already lift up your eyes and look upon it.

I have prepared this for you, and I have stood beside you through the times of endurance, and I have smiled, knowing what was in store for you. I have urged you on when you would have given up, because I would not allow you to fail.

Love Me more than ever. Recognize My hand in this.

Have no fear. Your work is My work, and I am well able to take care of every aspect.

How has God's hand worked in my life?

A Living Sacrifice

from *Come Away My Beloved*

And the three mighty men. . .drew water out of the well of
Bethlehem. . .and brought it to David: nevertheless he would
not drink thereof, but poured it out unto the LORD.

2 SAMUEL 23:16

*Y*ou are aware when My Spirit rejoices within you. This is
My joy. This is the joy I promised.

This is the greatest joy that can come to the human heart,
for it is the joy of God.

Surely you will not only rejoice but be exceeding glad, with
a gladness surpassing your power to tell.

In this way you will give this back to Me, even as David
poured out to Me the precious water from the well of Bethlehem.

Am I pouring out my praise to the Lord?

Give Me a Drink

from *Come Away My Beloved*

And Elijah said unto her, Fear not; go and do as thou hast
said: but make me thereof a little cake first, and bring it
unto me, and after make for thee and for thy son.

1 KINGS 17:13

*G*ive Me just a cupful of your limited affection. I long for it.
I weep for it as I wept for the love of Jerusalem. I will pour out
upon you such love as you have never known. Love that will
flood your whole being with such satisfaction as you never
dreamed possible to experience except in heaven. I beg of you,
"Give Me a drink." Or in the language of Elijah, "Make me a
small cake from it first" (1 Kings 17:13-16) and you will never
lack for meal and oil.

Does God have my affection?

Be Responsive

from *Progress of Another Pilgrim*

And he said, Go forth, and stand upon the mount before the
LORD. And, behold, the LORD passed by, and a great and strong
wind rent the mountains, and brake in pieces the rocks
before the LORD; but the LORD was not in the wind.

1 KINGS 19:11

*B*e responsive to the promptings of the Holy Spirit. I may
not speak with a blast of the trumpet. It may be a touch on the
shoulder. Do not wait for some climactic experience. Follow
the still, small voice. Be obedient to the gentle moving of My
Spirit. I often work this way because I want to develop your
sensitivity.

I know your frailties, but in this way I purpose to make you
strong. By working with you in this quiet fashion, I would
strengthen your faith.

Am I responding to His still, small voice?

Protection

from *On the Highroad of Surrender*

And the LORD opened the eyes of the young man;
and he saw: and, behold, the mountain was full of
horses and chariots of fire round about Elisha.

2 KINGS 6:17

*M*y protection is all you need, My child. The help of others is vain. But all will fall into place beautifully as you rest it in My hands. Fear not that any can harm you.

Gehazi owed his own safety to Elisha, for God was with Elisha in the form of an angelic host that filled the mountains, and Gehazi, the servant, benefited by being in his company. So shall it be for those who journey with you, as God, seeing your confidence in Him and desire to please Him and do His will, moves in your behalf.

Cast fear forever from your heart.

When have I experienced God's protection?

End-Time Tensions

from *On the Highroad of Surrender*

And it shall be, when you hear a sound of marching
in the tops of the mulberry trees, then you shall
go out to battle, for God has gone out before
you to strike the camp of the Philistines.

1 CHRONICLES 14:15 NKJV

*M*y grace and mercy are intensified, not in spite of, but
because of the tensions of the end-time. My love is moving in
surrendered hearts and producing a quality of dedication, zeal,
and awareness unsurpassed in the spiritual heroes of the past.

Lift up your heads: Lift up your hearts. Let your faith and
courage be reinforced. For in the Spirit you shall listen and
hear the sound of a great army readying for battle, and there
shall be the sound of going in the tops of the mulberry trees,
and they who have been enlisted by the Spirit shall go forth
conquering and to conqueror.

What role will I play in God's battle?

Motivation

from *Progress of Another Pilgrim*

If my people, which are called by my name, shall humble
themselves, and pray, and seek my face, and turn
from their wicked ways; then will I hear from heaven,
and will forgive their sin, and will heal their land.

2 CHRONICLES 7:14

*C*onfession, repentance, and prayer strengthen the will to
move in the direction of holiness. No one is brought into a life
of holiness by outside force. The inner desire is always the
first and the foremost motivation. As soon as the desire for
righteousness is present, the Holy Spirit will immediately fill
it with His own energy and bring the soul into victory.

What do I need to confess, repent of, and pray over?

Deliverance Has Come

from *Make Haste My Beloved*

And when they began to sing and to praise,
the LORD set ambushments against [their enemies].

2 CHRONICLES 20:22

*Y*es, and I have set ambushments against your enemies, and I will smite him that causes you to dwell in fear. I will not suffer your foot to be moved but will cause you to walk in the way I have designed for you and no man shall hinder. For I have set My battle in array, and I, the Lord your God, will fight for you and you shall hold your peace.

You shall rejoice and sing, yes, you can dance for joy, for your deliverance has already come, and the day of your visitation is here!

In what ways has God delivered me?

Devotion and Warfare

from On the Highroad of Surrender

> Every one of the builders had his sword
> girded at his side as he built. And the one
> who sounded the trumpet was beside me.
>
> NEHEMIAH 4:18 NKJV

*P*resume not to labor to build with the right hand without holding the sword in the left (Nehemiah 4:18). It is vigilance combined with prayer that spells victory. Devotion must be coupled with warfare to be fruitful. Holy ecstasy must be mixed with holy boldness, and love must be blended with courage. Only to pray is not enough. Prayer must rise from the battlefield of spiritual conquest.

How well do I handle God's "sword"—His Word?

Find Solitude

from *Come Away My Beloved*

Forty years You sustained them in the
wilderness; They lacked nothing.

NEHEMIAH 9:21 NKJV

*M*y Truth abides forever, and no one will escape, for it will be
as a flaming sword as it proceeds out of My mouth. For in judgment I will come, to purge the world and to set up My Kingdom.

Do not resist Me or harden your hearts. I take no pleasure
in the affliction of My children. In love I chasten to prevent
the deeper suffering involved should I allow you to go on in a
path of evil. But My heart is glad when you walk close, with
your hand in Mine, and we may talk over the plans for each
day's journey and activities so that it becomes a happy way
that we travel in mutual fellowship.

So pour out your praise to Me from a light heart. I will plan
your path, and we will go singing.

Is my heart hard or tender?

A Secret Process

from *On the Highroad of Surrender*

Every maid's turn was come to go in to king Ahasuerus,
after that she had been twelve months, according to
the manner of the women, (for so were the days of
their purifications accomplished.)

ESTHER 2:12

*M*y choicest saints often appear to escape chastening.
But I am perfecting inner beauty of the soul, as Esther was
prepared to meet the king by a full year of cosmetic routine
(Esther 2:12). I am doing a similar thing with My Church. My
Bride is undergoing her beautification in anticipation of the
coming of the Bridegroom.

This is why she must be drawn aside. This is a ministry to
her inner soul, and I have ordained special ones to carry out
this work of preparing the Bride. I commend you into their
hands and their ministrations. Only so can you be presented
before the King, purged of flaws and imperfections.

How has God beautified my soul?

I Have Built a Hedge

from *Progress of Another Pilgrim*

Hast not thou made an hedge about him,
and about his house, and about all that
he hath on every side?

JOB 1:10

*P*raise Me. Lift your heart in gratitude. In your sleeping and your waking hours, My hand of protection and blessing is upon you.

I have built a hedge about you, even as was written concerning Job. This was not a false accusation of the devil to Job: It was an actual reality. I only removed it to test and to prove him and to put to silence the enemy of his soul. But for multitudes of My children, I have never removed the hedge. I am keeping you, My child, and for one purpose in particular—that you be able to accomplish the task committed to you. Therefore, give diligence to your mission.

When has God placed a hedge around me?

An Uncomplaining Heart

from *On the Highroad of Surrender*

Behold, happy is the man whom God corrects;
Therefore do not despise the chastening of the Almighty.
For He bruises, but He binds up; He wounds,
but His hands make whole.

JOB 5:17-18 NKJV

---

*B*e patient while I deal with you in the areas of your own inner needs. Bear joyfully My rod of correction. Know that while I minister to you, you are being prepared to minister to others. Make no mistake, there cannot be one without the other. Your attitudes need the disciplining of the Holy Spirit.

Rest in Me in the quiet place and give Me an uncomplaining heart. I will fill it with My grace. When I see that you are ready to do it, I will make My will inescapable.

Are there complaints in my heart?

Affliction, No Stranger

from *On the Highroad of Surrender*

Though He slay me, yet will I trust Him.
Even so, I will defend my own ways before Him.

JOB 13:15 NKJV

———◆———◆———◆———

Affliction is no stranger to the child of God. I cannot spare you suffering. Grief and death are the experience of everyone, and darkness falls upon both saint and sinner. Those who know Me intimately will find a deep joy in the midst of life's bitterness. My Spirit dwelling within gives stamina in the face of hardship.

I do not smooth out the way for My loved ones, for how then could they testify of My provision? Better your lips were sealed forever than that they should deny Me in the hour of calamity.

I prepare you in order to use you in the hour of crisis. The crisis is not the time to cry for deliverance, saying, "Lord, save me," but to cry, "Lord, use me."

How does want to God use me?

Inner Calm

from *On the Highroad of Surrender*

Now acquaint yourself with Him, and be at peace;
Thereby good will come to you.

JOB 22:21 NKJV

*L*et nothing disturb your quietness of spirit, for from
the place of inner calm you draw courage to move forward
through all obstacles. I am never the source of turbulence. You
may react with turbulence when I am dealing with your soul,
but whenever you do so, it is because your will is in rebellion
and you have stiffened your neck. My disciplines are received
with peace in the heart that is submissive to My will.

Never console the one who pines under My chastening rod
lest you hinder the work of grace I am doing in his heart and
become an obstacle to his spiritual growth.

How well do I accept God's discipline?

The Simplicity of Obedience

from *Progress of Another Pilgrim*

And unto man he said, "Behold, the fear of the Lord,
that is wisdom, and to depart from
evil is understanding."

JOB 28:28 NKJV

*Y*ou need not search for answers to the many mysteries of
life, but only trust and follow Me in the simplicity of obedience.
Understanding will come to you as you walk in obedience.

Make Me your goal, and wisdom shall be given each day as
needed. Do not try to reverse the order.

What is my true goal in life?

Unseen Companionship

from On the Highroad of Surrender

Preserve me, O God, for in You I put my trust.

PSALM 16:1 NKJV

*C*ourage, My child! No hand shall sustain you but Mine own. Hoped you for another? Disappointment awaits every soul not sustained by My love. Never draw from other sources, for when you do, you rob the life force from another, leaving him weaker and yourself deceived; for you confuse comfort with strength.

Fellowship is not life. It is to be given rather than sought. It is shared in the overflow. The soul that has been enriched by communion with God will not be dismayed by isolation, but will welcome solitude. He will seek not the crowd but the closet, and emerging will never walk alone, for he has always unseen companionship, and whoever joins him on the way will be doubly blessed.

How have I been enriched by communion with God?

The Comfort of My Presence

from *On the Highroad of Surrender*

For You will light my lamp;
The Lord my God will enlighten my darkness.
For by You I can run against a troop,
And by God I can leap over a wall.

PSALM 18:28-29 NKJV

*O*ver and over have I reassured you of My love for you. More than all the comforts of the world, I want you to know the comfort of My presence.

Many dangers beset your path, but I shall keep you if you trust in Me. Many sorrows compass you about, but I give you joy that is greater. Darkness presses you, and doubts arise, but My light, the light of My Holy Spirit, ever burns within your heart to cheer you and encourage you to go on, yes, to go on knowing surely I will bring you out.

Do I have God's greater joy?

A Holy Temple

from *On the Highroad of Surrender*

Who may ascend into the hill of the LORD?
Or who may stand in His holy place?
He who has clean hands and a pure heart.

PSALM 24:3-4 NKJV

---

*Y*our heart, My child, is the citadel of the Holy Spirit. No evil shall dwell there as long as you allow Me to rule and reign. I hold the keys to every chamber and will keep out every evil thing if you do not invite the enemy. I desire for you a holy temple.

Let not your worship be tinged with carnality. Give Me your adoration from a pure heart and let no ulterior motives invade your personal sanctuary, for I desire truth in the depths of the soul, and the divided heart cannot worship.

How pure is my heart?

The Quiet Spirit

from *On the Highroad of Surrender*

Who may ascend into the hill of the LORD?
Or who may stand in His holy place?
He who has clean hands and a pure heart,
Who has not lifted up his soul to an idol,
Nor sworn deceitfully.
He shall receive blessing from the LORD,
And righteousness from the God of his salvation.

PSALM 24:3-5 NKJV

Be silent when you come to Me. Only the quiet spirit enters the place of communion. Strivings are left outside. Vexations bar the door, for they are caused by reactions to things, places, and people, and none of these are related to worship. They are related to the flesh. Put them out of the temple. They that have clean hands and a pure heart shall ascend unto the mountain of the Lord. When you are loosed from the earthly, then shall the heavenly be revealed.

What bars the door to my worship?

The Father's House

from *On the Highroad of Surrender*

One thing I have desired of the LORD,
That will I seek:
That I may dwell in the house of the LORD
All the days of my life,
To behold the beauty of the LORD,
And to inquire in His temple.

PSALM 27:4 NKJV

---

*I*n My Father's house are many mansions, and there is a place for you, My child. Look not for a place in the world. Your place is in the Father's house. Your soul can rest even now only in the place I provide.

Your restlessness is due to your involvement in things other than My ordained will for you. You are not of the world, even as I was not of the world. The spirit is nourished only by the eternal, and in prayer the soul breathes the atmosphere of heaven.

How much am I resting in the Father's will?

Angels Assist You

from *On the Highroad of Surrender*

I will extol You, O Lord, for You have lifted me up,
And have not let my foes rejoice over me. . . .
I cried out to You, And You have healed me.

PSALM 30:1-2 NKJV

My child, do not weep. I am doing a beautiful work. Stress and pressure and pain are often the path to victory and understanding.

I am in the midst, and I am a strong deliverer. You need not be concerned. Courage is the greatest contribution you can make at this point. To be strong now will make the path of recovery easier. Faith is an essential ingredient in every solution. . .often it is the solution itself.

Never underestimate the power of faith. Hold fast. Trust. Unseen angels assist you. Doors are opening to let you pass into safety.

Am I trusting God now?

Rejoice Always

from *On the Highroad of Surrender*

I will bless the Lord at all times;
His praise shall continually be in my mouth.

PSALM 34:1 NKJV

*K*nowing that I love you at all times will bring comfort in the hours when you need it most. Be obedient to My command that you rejoice in the Lord always. Because I must become your one true source of life and joy, I allow the difficult circumstances to come. Through them, I test your love for Me. It is not a time for you to test My love for you! My love for you is constant and is not to be reckoned by your own happiness or unhappiness. I send all in love. If you have unhappiness, it is because of your own wrong reactions.

Learn to react rightly and to properly discern My intention. Never blame Me for your misery, for it is not from My hand.

How can I discern God's intention?

Contentment

from *On the Highroad of Surrender*

Many are the afflictions of the righteous,
But the Lord delivers him out of them all.

PSALM 34:19 NKJV

*M*y children do not enjoy immunity to trouble, but in the midst of each painful experience My Spirit is at work fashioning beauty in the soul.

Be patient in tribulation and I will minister My grace to you and your heart will rejoice, yes, more than in the day of pleasantness. For when outer blessings are withheld, inner peace is deepened, for the soul turns to worship with less distraction.

Disappointment is foreign to the Spirit, for it has no part in faith. The trusting soul possesses all things in Christ and looks not to others for blessing: therefore, he can never be disappointed. Joy and contentment crown his head, and peace reigns in his heart.

Am I joyful and contented, or disappointed?

Loose the Child

from *On the Highroad of Surrender*

Cast your burden on the LORD,
And He shall sustain you;
He shall never permit the righteous to be moved.

PSALM 55:22 NKJV

The little ones are in My care; you shall not be anxious. He carries the lambs in His bosom. Surely, it is true. Rely on Me for I am ever watchful, and the tenderness of My love exceeds that of a mother.

Picture the Lord Jesus as He took the young children upon His knee and blessed them. I say to you, He is the same today, and His compassion fathomless. Trustingly place your child in His hands. They are healing hands, and you may count on Him to bring wholeness and perfection, whether here or in the Father's house.

Your heart is bound to the heart of the child. Loose the cord of affection lest it break.

Can I trust God with my child?

Trust

from *On the Highroad of Surrender*

In God I have put my trust;
I will not be afraid.
What can man do to me?

PSALM 56:11 NKJV

*Y*ou struggle, My child, when you could as easily rest in My arms. You concern yourself with the actions of others and neglect the only important thing: to abide in Me. He who abides in me has no need to be anxious.

When you are moving out of My divine will, you have unrest. Abiding brings confiding, for to know Me is to trust Me, and trust brings peace. Your trust in Me is colored by human experience. This should never be allowed to happen. Though all men fail, I am no less faithful: indeed, in the face of human disappointments your trust in Me becomes even more vital.

To understand is to believe, and to believe is to trust.

How vital is my trust in Him?

Living in Joy

from *On the Highroad of Surrender*

Let them be confounded and consumed who are
adversaries of my life; let them be covered with reproach
and dishonor who seek my hurt. But I will hope continually,
and will praise You yet more and more.

PSALM 71:13-14 NKJV

When you are baptized into His Spirit, evil loses its power
to destroy you, darkness is dispelled, and the broken spirit
healed. Joy is a balm that soothes the soul and lifts the burden
from the grieving heart. Joy will be your saving grace, and
praise your meat and drink. Only a joyful heart can worship
Me in a way pleasing in My sight.

To weep and mourn is needless waste.

Am I mourning or rejoicing today?

Maintain Constancy

from *On the Highroad of Surrender*

For He satisfies the longing soul,
And fills the hungry soul with goodness.

PSALM 107:9 NKJV

𝒟o not grieve, My child, though all you hold dear be taken from you. You have need of nothing. Hold Me close to your heart, and I will satisfy every longing. Allow Me to comfort you, and you will find yourself reaching out less and less to others for support and solace.

My presence will sustain you, but only if you maintain a closeness of relationship. Pure neglect alone can cause you to lose this as much as open sin.

Maintain a constancy in devotion, and I will be pleased and will do all manner of wonderful things in your behalf. I will cause blessings to be heaped upon you. You will be increased abundantly in the riches of the Kingdom.

How constant is my devotion?

The Romance of the Spirit

---

from *On the Highroad of Surrender*

Blessed are the undefiled in the way,
Who walk in the law of the LORD!
Blessed are those who keep His testimonies,
Who seek Him with the whole heart.

PSALM 119:1-2 NKJV

*T*here is a path of service in which I would lead you. No foot has preceded you there. It is virgin territory. It is My own special way for you. It is a way of romance—the Romance of the Spirit.

My love for you is deeper than you have comprehended. As you walk on into fuller commitment, and as you are less hampered by the things of the world, I will give you deeper insight and more complete revelations of Myself.

When you have given up everything, we will be able to go forth together, and you will experience an inner power that you were not able to find before.

How completely do I seek to serve God?

Harmony with the Message

from *On the Highroad of Surrender*

I will run in the way of Your commandments,
For You shall enlarge my heart.

PSALM 119:32 NKJV

I have many glorious things to reveal to you, but you must pay the price of treasuring, reverencing, and living in harmony with the message. Truth is always straightforward, and so also must be the one who receives it, or if he is not already, he must be willing to be made so.

You cannot perfect your own righteousness. I must do it for you, but I need your consent. I need your desire to be made holy. Surely I will answer when you call, and I will work in patience and in gentleness, but I will not stop until the perfecting process is finished.

Do I desire to be holy?

Constancy

from *On the Highroad of Surrender*

Indeed, the darkness shall not hide from You,
But the night shines as the day;
The darkness and the light are both alike to You.

PSALM 139:12 NKJV

---

*M*y child, My love, My little one, do not let your heart be discouraged. I am nearer to you than ever in the past. I have brought you up to a place of constancy, and I will hold you firm regardless of what you are feeling.

You do not need always to see My face to know I am near. You may touch My face to know I am near. You may touch My hand by faith in moments when it is too dark to see anything. Never let darkness frighten you. My Spirit is everywhere. . . even in the darkness.

When I fear, do I reach out to God or something else?

Trim Your Wick

---

from *On the Highroad of Surrender*

Search me, O God, and know my heart. . .
see if there is any wicked way in me,
and lead me in the way everlasting.

PSALM 139:23-24 NKJV

My child, do not that which I have not bidden. In My Name alone you ought to minister, and only when your own soul is free can the Spirit move unhindered.

Not only is time wasted when you disobey Me, but many souls are damaged, and your own no less.

Never try to evaluate a situation. Obey Me. It is difficult only to be obedient. How can you presume to handle any more?

Trim your wick and polish your lamp. Your light is growing dim. Come back to listening only to My voice.

I love you and I have chosen and trained you to do the tasks I have ordained. Be content with nothing less.

How obedient have I been to God?

Unquestioning Trust

from Progress of Another Pilgrim

Trust in the LORD with all thine heart;
and lean not unto thine own understanding.

PROVERBS 3:5

*L*et Me bless you. You need My blessing more than you need the help of all others combined. How often have I asked you to follow Me? I look to see you following, and instead I see you standing still and reckoning—or worse, fainting by the wayside.

It is your total commitment for which I wait. It is your unquestioning trust for which I yearn. It is your love flowing in utter simplicity which alone opens your channel to receive My mercies.

You can turn your burdens into blessings by giving Me everything.

Am I totally committed to God?

The Language of Love

from *On the Highroad of Surrender*

Keep your heart with all diligence,
For out of it spring the issues of life.

PROVERBS 4:23 NKJV

*B*e silent, My child, and when you speak, let it be your heart that calls My name. Many have My name upon their lips but their hearts are a hollow shell. Love is not in a mouth that is full, but in an overflowing heart.

With the heart man believes unto righteousness, and with the mouth he confesses unto salvation (Romans 10:10). No mouth shall testify of salvation and speak the truth until first the heart has believed unto righteousness.

I listen for the words of your heart. I understand the language of love.

When you listen for My voice, listen with your heart.

What do I need to "tune out" to hear God with my heart?

Do Not Gather Fire

from *On the Highroad of Surrender*

Can a man take fire to his bosom,
and his clothes not be burned?
PROVERBS 6:27 NKJV

❦

*H*ave I not said you should pray much that you might not
enter into temptation? You are in My care at all times, but
some stresses put upon the soul could be avoided by not pre-
suming upon My grace.

I desire always to help, but many pray too late; for by their
own careless actions they have placed their feet in a slippery
path, and the results are almost inevitable. Prayer at this
point is like seeking guidance when the route has been prede-
termined by self-will and the destination is already in sight.

Do not gather fire into your garments and pray not to be
burned, nor take up a serpent and ask for protection. Give the
devil wide berth, and spare the soul much unnecessary anguish.

How wide a berth have I given the devil?

Learn to Listen

from *On the Highroad of Surrender*

In the multitude of words sin is not lacking,
but he who restrains his lips is wise.

PROVERBS 10:19 NKJV

*W*hen you pray, My child, do not make it a one-way conversation. Know I am listening, but know also I will respond and will speak to you if you give Me opportunity. Prayer is not only of the lips, but of the ear also, for prayer is of the heart, and the heart that has learned to love has learned to listen more than to speak!

A loving heart will teach you this. Speaking is often motivated by self-seeking, self-preservation, self-defense, self-aggrandizement, and every other expression of the ego. Listening is an expression of interest and concern for others.

When you come to Me in prayer, you ought to come to enjoy Me, not to entertain Me. A lack of humility causes you to be verbally expansive.

Am I listening in prayer?

True Peace and False

from *Progress of Another Pilgrim*

There is a way which seemeth right unto a man,
but the end thereof are the ways of death.

PROVERBS 14:12

---

*P*eace is in the full expression of My will. Anything short of this is a false peace. There is a dullness of spirit. . .a sort of stupor that overtakes the one who is no longer spiritually sensitive. This is often mistaken for true peace in a way that can be compared to the freezing man who feels sleepy, not knowing he is slipping into the very jaws of death.

Let not this sort of thing befall you. Make sure that your peace is the result of actively being in the will of God, and permit yourself no indulgence in selfishness.

How much of God's peace am I experiencing?

Godly Sorrow Versus Carnal

from *Progress of Another Pilgrim*

A merry heart maketh a cheerful countenance:
but by sorrow of the heart the spirit is broken.

PROVERBS 15:13

*O*vermuch sorrow causes the heart to fail. If you would be a rejoicing Christian, the griefs of the carnal man must be laid aside. There are sufferings of spirit through which every soul must pass in the process of perfection, but these are not to be compared to the complaints laid upon the soul which are directly related to uncrucified affections.

To bemoan any unpleasant natural circumstance accomplishes nothing but a heaping up of misery. Undue distress about untoward happenings is devastating to the soul. The only kind of sorrow that I can use for your good is the godly sorrow of true repentance.

Turn to Me in every trial, and give it all to Me.

What trials are in my life today?

Frugality and Supply

from *Progress of Another Pilgrim*

Better is little with the fear of the LORD than
great treasure and trouble therewith.

PROVERBS 15:16

⸺⸻⸺

*Y*ou shall have My blessing as you bear the yoke, and in
carrying My burdens there shall always be joy. I have called
you for this ministry, and I will supply your needs so that you
will not be weighed down with financial cares. Be willing to
do without until I supply. Such as is needful I will give, and
anything more would be a snare and a disappointment.

Luxuries burden the soul with guilt. Learn to discern the
difference between necessities and luxuries, and be content
with modest things.

Leave off indulgences and follow the pattern of others who
have learned this lesson. Let your soul be inspired by the character of those who are disciplined in frugality.

How can I be disciplined in frugality?

A Merry Heart

from *On the Highroad of Surrender*

A merry heart does good, like medicine.

PROVERBS 17:22 NKJV

*T*o mourn adversity multiplies the misfortune. It is not hypocrisy to rejoice in distress: It is obedience, for, says the Scripture, "Rejoice in the Lord always and again I say, Rejoice" (Philippians 4:4).

Nothing is gained, but much is lost by bitterness of spirit in the day of trouble. You may not be able to escape calamity, but you should even more avoid a doleful countenance because it denotes a tempest in the heart and turbulence of mind, and reveals rebellion against the hand of God as it shapes destiny.

Look unto Jesus, "the author and finisher of our faith" (Hebrews 12:2). In Him dwells only that which is of the light. Peace, joy, and hope are His mantle, and holiness emanates from His presence.

Have I learned to rejoice in distress?

Wisdom, a Gift

from *On the Highroad of Surrender*

He who goes about as a talebearer reveals secrets;
Therefore do not associate with one who flatters with his lips.
PROVERBS 20:19 NKJV

*M*uch false doctrine has been generated out of man's fleshly desire to possess knowledge not yet revealed. In his impertinence, he has resented even the silence of God and expressed his intolerance of this silence by fabricating ideas of his own to fill the vacuum of ignorance.

O foolish creature! To have the mind filled with information is a questionable blessing. Knowledge and wisdom are gifts from God. Information wrongly acquired or inaccurately interpreted becomes a curse rather than a blessing. Be content to know only what is freely revealed by either God or man, and be not a scavenger of worthless information.

How am I using God's gifts of knowledge and wisdom?

Indolence

from *Progress of Another Pilgrim*

I went by the field of the slothful. . .it was all grown
over with thorns, and nettles had covered the face thereof,
and the stone wall thereof was broken down.

PROVERBS 24:30-31

*Y*ou could easily fill your days with frivolous or selfish pursuits. Guard your time and energies, as they are the material from which the spiritual ministries are of necessity channeled. Dissipate your physical strength, or carelessly waste your time, and thus shall the Spirit be thwarted. Simple indolence is by itself a militant force against the Spirit. Resist it in the full recognition of the destructive power that it is.

Determine in your heart to respond immediately to every prompting of the Spirit. Never dispute, for He is always right, and there can be no ramifications.

What kind of pursuits fill my days?

Withdraw Your Foot

from *On the Highroad of Surrender*

Where there is no wood, the fire goes out;
and where there is no talebearer, strife ceases.

PROVERBS 26:20 NKJV

---

*R*obbed of privacy, friendship is destroyed. Invade not the privacy of another life, nor probe where discretion has closed the door. There is a degree of reserve to which each soul has birthright, and which if relinquished to the curiosity of the impudent, leaves him stripped of the riches of his soul and robbed of his self-respect.

Beat not upon the closed door, nor contrive to be admitted where no invitation has been given.

The riches of friendship are placed in the hands of those who prove themselves trustworthy. The ignorant will rob a nest of its eggs. The wise wait patiently for the sound of baby birds. He who steals the eggs deprives himself of this pleasure.

What kind of friend am I?

Inner Strength and Outer Action

from *Progress of Another Pilgrim*

He that covereth his sins shall not prosper:
but whoso confesseth and forsaketh
them shall have mercy.

PROVERBS 28:13

*I*ntegrity and devotion have always been indispensable virtues. I say to you that in this hour of apathy and decline when the very foundations of mankind's moral structures are crumbling, you need to be more diligent than ever to find and to keep your own personal inner strength and to allow it to manifest in outer action.

How much integrity and devotion characterize my life?

A Yielded Spirit

from *On the Highroad of Surrender*

He who is often reproved, and hardens his neck,
will suddenly be destroyed, and that without remedy.

PROVERBS 29:1 NKJV

---

*T*he lesson of obedience is still of first importance. Unless you move in obedience, all your other actions and your knowledge will be misdirected and unfruitful. Know My will, and do it. But, you say, How can I know God's will? I have revealed it to you, My child, and I am constantly seeking to guide you in myriad ways. Your self-will blots out My divine directives. Before the sound of My voice registers on your consciousness, you drown it out with the objections of an unyielded spirit. You will never move freely in My highest purpose unless you constantly offer up to Me a yielded, broken, self-renouncing vessel.

Am I a yielded vessel?

Bread Upon the Waters

from *Come Away My Beloved*

Cast your bread upon the waters,
for you will find it after many days.

ECCLESIASTES 11:1 NKJV

Do not be afraid to follow Me, nor draw back in doubt. I will provide all that you lack, and I will pave the way for you with My bounty.

You are not treading alone. There are many with you on the same road. It is the road of faith and trust, and you will have sweet fellowship, for there are others who will join you in this walk.

You will rejoice with exceeding joy, and your joy shall be shared by angels. They walk beside you and guard your way.

Never limit Me. I will take you through, though cliffs should rise before you. There will always be a provision, and in My mercy I will see that you find it.

How has God provided for me during my Christian walk?

Praise and Reproof

from *Come Away My Beloved*

Behold, you are fair, my love!
Behold, you are fair!
SONG OF SOLOMON 1:15 NKJV

—◦—◦—◦—

*M*y child, do not let the words of others influence you unduly—neither their praise nor their criticism. Weigh each for its proper value, and come back to Me. Only in communion with Me can you be sure of the truth. If I correct you, it is for your betterment. If I encourage you, it is because I know you need it.

If you accept My love and approval, you will be given courage to face your sins and faults. The more you find of the truth about your own self, the more you will be set free from improper evaluations of your worth, free from false pride that seeks to cover recognized flaws.

I want your life, character, and personality to be as beautiful and lovely as I visualized you to be when I created you.

Have I truly accepted God's love and approval?

God's Heart

from *Come Away My Beloved*

My beloved spake, and said unto me,
Rise up, my love, my fair one, and come away.
SONG OF SOLOMON 2:10

I love you, and if you can always, as it were, feel My pulse beat, you will receive insight that will give you sustaining strength. I bore your sins and I wish to carry your burdens. You may take the gift of a light and merry heart, for My love dispels all fear and is a cure for every ill. Lay your head upon My breast and lose yourself in Me. You will experience resurrection life and peace; the joy of the Lord will become your strength, and wells of salvation will be opened within you (see Song of Solomon 2:9-13).

Are the wells of salvation opened in me?

Immediate Obedience

from *On the Highroad of Surrender*

If you are willing and obedient,
you shall eat the good of the land.
ISAIAH 1:19 NKJV

*Y*ou never enhance either your own life nor the lives of others if you are out of My perfect will. When I give you guidance and you are persuaded in your own mind of My leading, never ponder your decision. There is but one possible reply, and that is "Yes, Lord." Then simply do My bidding, and do it immediately.

Much confusion and remorse would be averted if all My children acted in this manner. This is why delayed obedience is nearly always disobedience, because along with the procrastination there is deliberation followed by rationalization, and by the time decision finally evolves into action, your own will is in control.

How often do I delay my obedience?

The Seeds of the Word

from *Progress of Another Pilgrim*

I heard the voice of the Lord, saying,
Whom shall I send, and who will go for us?
Then said I, Here am I; send me.

ISAIAH 6:8

Lo, the message is Mine, but I have need of those who will speak it without alteration and without any attempt to please men.

I have much to say that is not pleasant to hear, because the heart of man has grown fat with self-interest, and the light of the knowledge of the things of God has grown dim.

The seeds of the Word have long since dried up and died in many a prayerless life. I need those who will speak it again and send it out afresh in the dynamic power of the Holy Spirit. The Word must be spoken through those who are spiritually alive; otherwise, it loses its power to produce new life.

Am I willing to accurately speak God's truth?

Learn Well and Listen Closely

from *Progress of Another Pilgrim*

Thou wilt keep him in perfect peace, whose mind
is stayed on thee: because he trusteth in thee.

ISAIAH 26:3

———

*N*o disturbance, either in yourself or in others, can interfere with the moving of My Spirit if you do not focus attention
upon it.

Be as a babe in its mother's arms and know that I carry you
near to My heart, and this is why you have knowledge of many
things not revealed to others. They must find this place for
themselves before they can hear My voice. Meanwhile, you are
My ambassador to them.

Learn well, and listen closely.

What kind of an ambassador have I been for God?

An Instrument of Praise

from *Come Away My Beloved*

In returning and rest you shall be saved;
In quietness and confidence shall be your strength.

ISAIAH 30:15 NKJV

My child, I have chosen you for Myself, that I may make you an instrument of praise in My hand. I will bring forth from you a melody of praise and rejoicing, and cause the harp strings of your soul to vibrate with a joyful song.

Bless Me with your lips, and whisper My Name in adoration. I will free you from the prison house, and you will exalt your God in liberty of spirit.

Do not turn back in unbelief, but press onward and upward until the darkness is left behind and you come out into the light. You will see Me then face-to-face, and know Me as your dearest friend.

What kind of praise instrument am I?

Release Your Tensions

from *On the Highroad of Surrender*

The work of righteousness will be peace, and the effect of
righteousness, quietness and assurance forever.

ISAIAH 32:17 NKJV

The path to holiness is strewn with many heartaches. I
bring you through victoriously, but I do not promise that you
will escape suffering.

When you are rebuffed and bear it patiently, yes, even in
the moment when it appears as though the actions of others
prevent the fulfillment of your own inner vision, be assured,
My child, of My understanding and patience, and know that I
am a harmonizing influence.

Even your zeal to please Me should never destroy another.
Bless him, and know that it is possible that he may be fulfilling
My purposes for him even though it seems he is hindering your
own spiritual expression. I have a unique plan for each life, and as
you release to Me your tensions, you can rely on Me to continue
My work in each soul and bring it ultimately to perfection.

What tensions should I release to God?

Heaven's Gift

from *On the Highroad of Surrender*

My people will dwell in a peaceful habitation,
in secure dwellings, and in quiet resting places.

ISAIAH 32:18 NKJV

———•—•———•—•———•—•———

Quietness of soul, My child, is heaven's rarest gift enjoyed aforetime. It is unknown to the sinner, for there is no peace to the wicked, but only stress and restlessness. To abide in Me is to know release from tensions, and the ear that is attuned to My voice does not respond to chaos.

People assault their ears with noise to drown the cry of their souls for help. All too often they choose to perpetuate their own misery rather than repent of their evil ways and accept the rulership of another who is greater than themselves.

How well do I abide in God's peace?

The Call of Love

from *Come Away My Beloved*

Wisdom and knowledge will be the stability
of your times, and the strength of salvation.

ISAIAH 33:6 NKJV

My beloved, abide under the shelter of the lattice for I have betrothed you to Myself, and though you are sometimes indifferent toward Me, My love for you is at all times as a flame of fire. My ardor never cools. My longing for your love and affection is deep and constant.

Tarry not for an opportunity to have more time to be alone with Me. Take it, though you leave the tasks at hand. Nothing will suffer. Things are of less importance than you think. Our time together is like a garden full of flowers, whereas the time you give to things is as a field full of stubble.

Am I growing a garden or creating a stubble-filled field?

Ask!

from *Come Away My Beloved*

The parched ground shall become a pool,
and the thirsty land springs of water.

ISAIAH 35:7 NKJV

If there is dryness within your soul and you do not have this life flowing forth, you need not grieve or chide yourself for being empty. Fill up the empty place with praise. Through praise you may open the gates to your soul's temple. The King will enter and bring His glory

For the promise of the Father is the gift of the indwelling presence of My Holy Spirit, promised to all who have been baptized in the name of Jesus Christ, who have repented of their sins and received remission (see Acts 2:38).

Yes, I say to you, it is a gift. It is written: "How much more will your heavenly Father give the Holy Spirit to those who ask Him" (Luke 11:13 NKJV)! Ask, and you shall receive, and your joy shall be full.

Have I received God's gift of His Spirit?

Do Not Lie Dormant

from *Come Away My Beloved*

But those who wait on the Lord
Shall renew their strength;
They shall mount up with wings like eagles,
They shall run and not be weary,
They shall walk and not faint.

ISAIAH 40:31 NKJV

My child, I need you. Without your active help, I am hampered in My work. You cannot lie idle without hindering the ministry of the Church as a corporate body. You cannot move independently of My Spirit without causing damage to the harmonious working of the whole; for by My Spirit is oneness of thought and action produced. Never be dormant. Do not be slothful, neither let yourself fall asleep.

I am with you, and I will help you. Do not become discouraged or weary or fainthearted, and you will reap My rewards.

Am I discouraged and weary, or waiting on the Lord?

Rivers of Living Water

from *Come Away My Beloved*

When the poor and needy seek water. . .
And their tongues fail for thirst,
I, the LORD, will hear them;
I. . .will not forsake them.
I will open rivers in desolate heights,
And fountains in the midst of the valleys;
I will make the wilderness a pool of water,
And the dry land springs of water.

ISAIAH 41:17-18 NKJV

*B*ehold, you are in the hollow of My hand. In the moment that you lift your voice to cry out to Me, then shall My glory gather you up. Yes, I shall wrap you in the garments of joy, and My presence shall be your great reward.

Lift your eyes to Mine. You shall know without a doubt that I love you. Lift your voice to Me in praise; in this way a fountain shall be opened within you, and you will drink of its refreshing waters.

When have I drunk from God's fountain?

Stay Beneath My Wing

from *Come Away My Beloved*

When you pass through the waters, I will be with you;
And through the rivers, they shall not overflow you.
When you walk through the fire, you shall not be burned,
Nor shall the flame scorch you.

ISAIAH 43:2 NKJV

*M*y people: Will I create, and will I not have it in My power to destroy? Is it not written that the potter breaks one vessel that He may shape a new one (see Jeremiah 18:4)? Yes, I will bring My will to pass, and man will know that his will is like a broken straw when pitted against the Almighty.

But My people will know the protection of their God. If I removed you from the scene, you would have no testimony of My miraculous delivering power. Stay beneath My wings, and I will make you a tower of strength to which the fearful may run and find safety.

Am I a strong tower for God?

Why Do You Falter?

from Progress of Another Pilgrim

I will go before thee, and make the
crooked places straight.

ISAIAH 45:2

---

*O*My child, I have need of you. Have I not called you and blessed you? Have I not laid My hand upon you and shaped you for My purposes? Why, then, do you doubt?

It is only patterns of the past that bind your thoughts. They can exert no power over tomorrow except as you deliberately give them life. With every task I assign, I also give the enablement.

I have tested your faith many times, and I know it is strong. Why do you falter? Rise, and go in My Name, knowing it is I who thrust you forth. It is not man. This is My plan for you. The way should be easy when you know this.

What is God's testing accomplishing in my life?

Submission and Redemption

from *Progress of Another Pilgrim*

Behold, I have refined thee, but not with silver;
I have chosen thee in the furnace of affliction.

ISAIAH 48:10

*D*eath is swallowed up in victory only for the man who has committed fully into the hands of the Father his total being. Be not deceived when confronted by the darkness. Out of the hour of temptation comes the light of My transforming work in your soul.

You have asked to be freed of sin and drawn closer to Me. Trust Me now, as I do My perfecting work.

Lean upon My heart. I take no pleasure in afflicting your soul. I desire always for you a speedy deliverance. You help to bring it as you trust Me and as you yield your soul to whatever instrument I use for the accomplishment of My work in you (Romans 7:24-25).

How much have I yielded my heart to God's work?

Preparation

from *Progress of Another Pilgrim*

Thus saith the LORD. . .I am the LORD thy God
which teacheth thee to profit, which leadeth
thee by the way that thou shouldest go.

ISAIAH 48:17

No event in your life is a mistake. I will use every circumstance to enrich your ministry and perfect your soul. You shall go because I have need of you, and minister in the full power of your calling.

You shall go not by man's bidding, but I shall thrust you forth. Be not surprised, neither question how it shall come to pass. The opening of doors is My responsibility, but the preparation of your soul is your own responsibility.

If you would be ready when the time comes, be diligent and follow My guidance in every detail. You are not pampering the flesh but strengthening the body that it may be an adequate vehicle to carry the Spirit.

Am I an adequate vehicle for His Spirit?

The Heavenly Quest

from *Make Haste My Beloved*

He is despised and rejected of men;
a man of sorrows, and acquainted with grief.

ISAIAH 53:3

---

*M*any heartaches come to those who follow Me. Some are common to all men; others are the direct result of simply being a disciple of one who Himself was called "a man of sorrows, and acquainted with grief" (Isaiah 53:3). If you are obedient to Me, you will experience a similar kind of suffering, the suffering of spiritual sacrifice. It is not self-sacrifice, for it is not a giving of self, per se. It is a new and more stringent kind of dedication—it is the heavenly quest for total abandonment to the will of God.

Have I truly abandoned myself to God?

The Glory Life

from *Dialogues with God*

For my thoughts are not your thoughts,
neither are your ways my ways, saith the LORD.

ISAIAH 55:8

*L*ean upon Me for wisdom, yea, lean wholly upon Me, for thou knowest not the direction of thyself, but it shall be revealed unto thee by My Spirit, saith the Lord.

Day by day and step by step, thou shalt walk by faith, not by thine own cunningly devised plans.

I desire to do a new thing. How canst thou discover it?

If thou couldst, thou wouldst spoil the thrill of it, as a child finding his gift before the time.

Question Me not, nor ask Me why, neither put confidence in the wisdom of thine own thoughts.

I will never fail thee nor lead thee astray.

I will accomplish that which I purpose.

Am I leaning on God's wisdom or seeking my own?

I Will Use but Not Destroy You

from *Come Away My Beloved*

So shall My word be that goes forth from My mouth;
It shall not return to Me void.

ISAIAH 55:11 NKJV

My child, do not be overcharged with the cares of everyday living, and do not let your energies be consumed by humdrum tasks. What is needed must be done; but if you put the ministry of the Kingdom in first place, My strength will be yours for other tasks, and time will be given to you for both.

You do not need to respond to every call. Learn to discern when I would use you, and when I would have the other individual lean wholly upon Me.

I will use you, but I will not destroy you in the using. But you may destroy yourself if you lack this discernment and fail to know when to direct others to look to Me.

What daily cares have taken my eyes off the Lord?

I Do Not Send Storms

from *Progress of Another Pilgrim*

There is no peace, saith my God, to the wicked.

ISAIAH 57:21

*Dear Jesus, in the hollow of Thy
hand there is peace.*

*Y*es, My child, but do not ask Me to give you peace when you have removed yourself from My hand or if you are unwilling to rest quietly there. I give My peace to all who love and serve Me with singleness of heart. Any duplicity either in character or in aim shall bring disquiet.

I do not *send* storms upon your soul. They are generated by the pressures of your disobedience.

Only in repentance shall my people find peace, and only in singleness of heart shall they find joy.

Am I in a place where God can give me peace?

A Garden of Fountains

from *Come Away My Beloved*

The LORD will guide you continually,
And satisfy your soul in drought,
And strengthen your bones;
You shall be like a watered garden,
And like a spring of water, whose waters do not fail.

ISAIAH 58:11 NKJV

---

*B*ehold, My hand is upon you to bless you and to accomplish all My good purpose. For this hour I have prepared your heart, and in My kindness I will not let you fail.

Only relinquish all things into My hands; for I can work freely only as you release Me by complete committal—both of yourself and others. As was written of old: "Commit your way to the LORD, trust also in Him, and He shall bring it to pass" (Psalm 37:5 NKJV). I will be your sustaining strength, and My peace shall garrison your mind. Only trust Me—all I do is done in love.

What do I need to relinquish to God?

A Devouring Fire

from *On the Highroad of Surrender*

When the enemy comes in like a flood,
the Spirit of the LORD will lift up a standard against him.
ISAIAH 59:19 NKJV

Be prepared, O My people, and know that darkness is ever moving against My Church. It moves against you as a believer, but I have promised to deliver, and he who walks in prayer shields his soul from the enemy.

Hold forth the word of truth, both receiving it and giving it, for it is a devouring fire as it goes forth against evil. Lo, it is written, that when I come, I shall destroy the wicked with the words of My mouth (Revelation 19:15, Hebrews 4:12). You shall be able to scatter much darkness and combat the powers of evil as you speak My Word in faith.

How prepared am I to face the darkness?

Cleanse the Sanctuary

from *Come Away My Beloved*

For My people have committed two evils: They have forsaken
Me, the fountain of living waters, and hewn themselves
cisterns—broken cisterns that can hold no water.

JEREMIAH 2:13 NKJV

I have commanded that you love Me with a whole heart, and
that you serve Me with undivided loyalty. You cannot serve
two masters. Cleanse the sanctuary, and bring Me your sacrifices with pure hearts and clean hands. I will not despise the
sacrifices of contrite hearts.

I long after you with a love that embraces Eternity. Though
you go astray, I will surely draw you back. When you turn to
Me, I shall bridge the gap. Although you have strayed, I have
not left you. Wherever you turn to Me in love and confession, I
am there in the midst of you.

Do I love God with a whole heart?

The Armor of Light

from *Progress of Another Pilgrim*

O Lord, I know that the way of man is not in himself:
it is not in man that walketh to direct his steps.

JEREMIAH 10:23

O My child, I call you to surrender. No problem confronts you that I cannot resolve. Given the opportunity, I will spare you disappointment and regret. Confess, and I will forgive, and I will extricate you from this situation that you have brought upon yourself.

You ran ahead of Me and fell into a snare. I will go with you Myself and make the crooked places straight and we will go on again, together. This time you will wait for My leading.

Wear the armor of the Spirit, and you have My protection. Fear not what others can do to harm you. Fear only your own tendency to act independently.

In what ways do I tend to act independently of God?

To Feel Need Is to Receive Grace

from *Make Haste My Beloved*

Call unto me, and I will answer thee, and shew thee
great and mighty things, which thou knowest not.

JEREMIAH 33:3

---

*M*y mercy flows in the stream of all your woes, My child.
No obstacle within yourself can restrict My grace. I use many
vessels while they are struggling with their failures; for in
their conscious sense of need, they are more yielded to Me
than they who think themselves to be without flaw. Nothing
restricts the Spirit's work more than the smug satisfaction of
the spiritually proud.

To feel need is to receive grace. The mighty things which
you do not comprehend are the miraculous things I do for you
and through you in your acknowledged times of need. I act in
and through you according to My grace and My own ability.

Do I feel the need for His grace?

Be Thou My Door of Hope

from On the Highroad of Surrender

It is of the LORD's mercies that we are not consumed,
because his compassions fail not. They are new
every morning: great is thy faithfulness.

LAMENTATIONS 3:22-23

*O*ut of the depths you have cried unto Me. I am gracious and
full of compassion. My heart is touched by the feeling of your
infirmities, and I am acquainted with your grief (Hebrews 4:15).

I am your help, for to whom else shall you go? I will be your
Door of Hope, though darkness is round about you.

Is God my only door of hope?

Eternity and Time

from *Come Away My Beloved*

A wheel in the middle of a wheel.

EZEKIEL 1:16

---

*B*ehold, a new day is dawning! Do not let the sound of war and discords deafen your ears to My message, for I would speak to you a word of encouragement and would bring you tidings of hope.

My little children, I have not gone away never to return; but I will surely come, yes, even at a time when you least expect.

Do not focus on the problems of the world, but look up, for surely your deliverance is near.

My ageless purposes are set in Eternity. Time is like a little wheel set within the big wheel of Eternity. The little wheel turns swiftly and shall one day cease. The big wheel turns not, but goes straightforward. Time is your responsibility– Eternity is Mine!

How well do I keep eternity in mind
as I spend my earthly time?

I Will Share My Secrets

from *Make Haste My Beloved*

He revealeth the deep and secret things: he knoweth what
is in the darkness, and the light dwelleth with him.

DANIEL 2:22

I will share with you My secrets
And reveal the hidden thing.
I will lift you out of darkness—
Understanding will I bring.
If you seek Me in My fullness
And desire to know My heart,
I will open heaven's riches
And My wisdom I'll impart.
I have not ordained My children
To be blind, uncomprehending:
I will be the light eternal,
Revelation to you sending.
For 'twas sin that brought the darkness,
And 'tis sin that blinds the soul,
But the blood of the atonement
Opens eyes and makes men whole.

What secrets has God been sharing with me?

In the Fiery Furnace

from *Progress of Another Pilgrim*

He answered and said, Lo, I see four men loose,
walking in the midst of the fire, and they have no hurt;
and the form of the fourth is like the Son of God.

DANIEL 3:25

*I*n a multitude of circumstances the soul is tested. Modern
man has so protected himself from discomfort and from un-
pleasantness that his body and his soul are in a dangerously
weakened condition. Where shall he draw courage in the day
of affliction?

Never try to smooth out the way for either yourself or another unless you have been definitely led to do so. Always you
need My guidance, even for your acts of benevolence.

Look for Me in the midst of every fiery furnace and you will
be influenced by My Spirit rather than by your own natural
impulses (2 Corinthians 11:16–32; 2 Timothy 2:3).

Where do I look when I face the furnace?

The Coward Seeks Release

from *On the Highroad of Surrender*

And the princes, governors, and captains, and the king's
counsellors, being gathered together, saw these men,
upon whose bodies the fire had no power, nor was an
hair of their head singed, neither were their coats changed,
nor the smell of fire had passed on them.

DANIEL 3:27

*H*old fast, My child, for in the hour of anguish, then shall
you walk in victory. Do not pray to be brought out of the fire
until after you have found Me real in the midst of it.

The coward seeks release from pressure. The courageous
pray for strength to overcome the evil force.

What am I praying for today?

Liberty

from *On the Highroad of Surrender*

All of whose works are truth, and His ways justice.
And those who walk in pride He is able to put down.

DANIEL 4:37 NKJV

---

*S*tand fast in the liberty wherein I have made you free and allow no one to move you into a position of compromise. Be diligent to make the most of the opportunities thus afforded you, and do not miss any.

You will never discover what I have planned for you if in your zeal you run ahead and become again entangled. I free you and I want to keep you free. Why do you look to others for help when I am already at work moving mountains, opening doors, and touching hearts on your behalf?

Be at peace.

How free is my life?

Faith Manifesting in Divine Response

from *Progress of Another Pilgrim*

My God hath sent his angel, and hath shut the lions' mouths,
that they have not hurt me: forasmuch as before him
innocency was found in me; and also before thee,
O king, have I done no hurt.

DANIEL 6:22

*N*o evil can hurt you if you yield it up to Me, because as you do so, I bring to bear upon it forces of good. One example in the Bible is the visitation of angels for the preservation of Daniel as he was cast into the den of lions. The power of righteousness at work within the heart of Daniel brought to his aid the protecting forces. It was faith and committal manifesting into divine response.

The same law will work for you. Test it and prove it. You will find that your fear of calamity will gradually be dissolved, and you will gain a firmer inner confidence.

How can I yield evil up to God?

A Yielded, Believing Vessel

from *Come Away My Beloved*

But the people who know their God shall be strong,
and carry out great exploits.

DANIEL 11:32 NKJV

*M*ine is the wisdom and the honor and the power and the glory and shall be so forever and ever. I make the nations rise and kingdoms fall, but My throne shall be established in Zion and My righteousness throughout all the earth.

I am never defeated, but My justice and My mercy are obstructed by human ignorance and by the lack of faith in even My children.

Be aware of Me. I can accomplish great things through even one yielded, believing vessel. Remember David, and how I wrought a great victory for the armies of Israel through his courage when all others were paralyzed by fear.

Move on, and never entertain the thought of retreat.

Where am I moving for God?

Comfort in Affliction

from *Come Away My Beloved*

Then they will seek My face;
In their affliction they will earnestly seek Me.

HOSEA 5:15 NKJV

𝒪 My people, has not My hand fashioned for you many signs and wonders? Have I not ministered to you in miraculous ways? How is it you say therefore in your heart, "I will turn again to human strength"? Will you not, then, trust Me now in this new emergency, even as you have trusted Me in the past?

Lean hard upon Me, for I bring you through to new victories, and restoration shall follow what seems now to be a wind of destruction. Draw upon the resources of My grace. Heaven rejoices when you go through trials with a singing spirit.

Be like a beacon light. His own glorious radiance shall shine through you, and Christ Himself will be revealed.

What kind of beacon am I for my Savior?

Grace

---

from *Progress of Another Pilgrim*

Then shall we know, if we follow on to know the LORD:
his going forth is prepared as the morning;
and he shall come unto us as the rain,
as the latter and former rain unto the earth.

HOSEA 6:3

---

*F*ollow righteousness, and pursue it with unmitigated fervor. It is the only pursuit that is legitimate for the Christian. I have given My promise that I will supply every other need if you seek righteousness. It is in the selfless abandon to the Spirit that grace is nurtured.

I have freely extended My grace to you. Now I desire to see My grace developed in you!

How is God's grace being developed in me?

Sound the Trumpet

from *On the Highroad of Surrender*

Blow the trumpet in Zion, and sound an alarm in
My holy mountain! Let all the inhabitants of the land tremble:
for the day of the LORD is coming, for it is at hand.

JOEL 2:1 NKJV

*B*e alert. Be vigilant. Sound the alarm from My holy mountain. Challenge my people that they be not overtaken by the
enemy because they have a false sense of security. By My
Spirit you shall overcome, and by My Word you shall prevail.

Gird on the armor of My holiness, and speak the word of
faith. Fear not the enemy, for he has already been stripped of
his power, and victory is yours. Surely I will send My delivering angel to stand beside you, and you shall not turn back,
neither give in to weariness, for the Lord your God, He is your
strength, and in His hand is the reward.

How alert and vigilant am I?

The Harvest Is Overripe

from *Progress of Another Pilgrim*

Put ye in the sickle, for the harvest is ripe: come,
get you down; for the press is full, the fats overflow;
for their wickedness is great.

JOEL 3:13

*T*he hour is late. Be diligent. The harvest is overripe, and because it is so, there is need for greater care in the gathering of it. Do not be presumptuous. Do not rely on the same kind of methods you used in the past. There is need for greater tenderness. There is need for greater compassion. There is need for infinite patience. This is a delicate work. When you deal with the souls of men, you are touching the most precious thing there is. No work is more demanding of wisdom. Seek Me continually for direction and for understanding, so that you may be able to gather the overripe fruit without bruising it.

What can I do to help harvest the fruit of souls?

The Golden Path

from *Progress of Another Pilgrim*

Surely the Lord G OD will do nothing, but he revealeth
his secret unto his servants the prophets.

A MOS 3:7

*My child, I have a special path for you. Search it out dili-
gently. Let Me guide you in it. Follow not other sheep aimlessly
as they roam through My pastures. Lo, I call you to follow me.

I have you on a path which is all your own. It is not My way
for anybody else. It will become clear to you only by revelation. This can only come from Me.

I call it the golden path. It is the golden path for you. It is a
sacred secret between us. Guard it and keep it, and treasure it
in the secret places of your soul.

Am I walking on God's golden path for me?

These Are Days of the Moving of My Spirit

from *Come Away My Beloved*

"Behold, the days are coming," says the Lord God,
"That I will send a famine on the land, not a famine of bread,
nor a thirst for water, but of hearing the words of the Lord."

AMOS 8:11 NKJV

Be alert. Be on guard. Do not attempt to make a judgment as to who is hungry for more of God. At any moment an appetite long dormant may be aroused, and the longer it has been dormant, the more voracious it will be.

Give My Word—these are the days of the moving of My Spirit; will you resist if I wish to make you My aqueduct?

Stay clear—allow no constriction nor obstruction, and do not be stingy. Growth will spring forth wherever the waters reach.

What obstructions may be blocking
the Spirit's flow in my life?

Gentleness

from *Progress of Another Pilgrim*

He hath shewed thee, O man, what is good;
and what doth the LORD require of thee, but to do justly,
and to love mercy, and to walk humbly with thy God?

MICAH 6:8

*B*e obedient to My commands: so shall I bless you. Let Me guide you: thus shall you know the right path. Follow always the call of the Spirit. All who listen shall hear. Move with the flexibility of a yielded will. Mercies are laid up in store for the humble.

Gentleness of spirit brings overcoming power. It is not the strong will, but the yielded will that is blessed in My sight.

How much am I yielding my will to God?

New Songs in Your Mouth

from *Come Away My Beloved*

But unto you that fear my name shall the Sun of
righteousness arise with healing in his wings;
and ye shall go forth, and grow up as calves of the stall.

MALACHI 4:2

O my soul, wait upon God, and He will do you good. Yes, He
will refresh your soul.

For His tender mercies are never failing, and His kindness
toward you is as the morning. As the Sun of Righteousness
shall arise with healing in His wings (see Malachi 4:2), so
shall your God be unto you.

For the night is past; yes, I bring you into a new place: a
place of rejoicing in Me such as you have not known as yet.

For I shall fill your soul with fatness, and I will be with you
to do you good.

What am I rejoicing about today?

The Attribute of Mercy

from *Progress of Another Pilgrim*

Blessed are the merciful: for they shall obtain mercy.

MATTHEW 5:7

*M*ercy is one of My attributes which I strongly desire you to have.

If you are not merciful, it would have been better had you not presumed to become My disciple. Without this quality in ministry, there can be no genuine blessing flowing through your life. In each relationship with others, if you do not have mercy, you will blight, not bless.

Without mercy, Calvary would have become a preachment of condemnation rather than of forgiveness. Expressing, as He did, His mercy toward His enemies, He provided you an example of the extent to which your own compassion should operate. You may never achieve an expression of love in the same degree, but let it be always the measure and the guide by which you judge your own attitudes.

In what ways can I show more mercy?

The Blessings of the Pure in Heart

from *Come Away My Beloved*

Blessed are the pure in heart:
for they shall see God.
MATTHEW 5:8

———•—+—•—+—•———

*I*s not My heart drawn out toward you to bless you? Have I not said that I would shelter and protect you and be your strong support? Yield your whole being to Me. I am your loving Father. I know your need even before it arises. My provisions are not only sure, but also full and overflowing, so that you may confess with the psalmist, "I shall never want." You will see with a vision denied to many, for your heart is pure, and to the pure of heart is given the promise that they shall see God. How much more glorious than to behold the beauty of a thousand sunsets! How much more thrilling than the sight of the fairest faces ever to grace the earth!

Do I delight in the thought of seeing God?

Chastening

from *Come Away My Beloved*

Ye are the salt of the earth: but if the salt have lost his savour,
wherewith shall it be salted? it is thenceforth
good for nothing, but to be cast out,
and to be trodden under foot of men.

MATTHEW 5:13

*H*ave I not said that unless you experience chastening, you may well doubt your sonship? Why then should you shrink from My rod of correction? You are not the teacher, but the pupil; not the parent, but the child; not the vine, but the branch.

Discipline and correction must come if you desire to be brought into conformity to My divine will. Shun nothing My hand brings to bear upon your life. Accept My blessings and My comfort, but do not despise My stern dealings. All are working toward your ultimate perfection.

In what ways has God been chastening me?

On Not Resisting Evil

from On the Highroad of Surrender

But I say unto you, That ye resist not evil:
but whosoever shall smite thee on thy right cheek,
turn to him the other also.

MATTHEW 5:39

---

*M*y wisdom will come to you, My child, when you become quiet. Anxiety places the soul in stress. The strivings of your own heart will be as out of harmony with My Spirit as the evil you wish to combat. This is why the scripture says, "Resist not evil."

You cannot correct the crooked path of another, but you can let Me show you how to make a straight path of your own. Never fear the darkness. . .avoid it.

Do not use your energy destroying the house of your enemy. If it is an unsound structure, it will eventually fall. You need your full attention to build rightly your own.

How often am I quiet before the Lord?

Come into the Secret Chambers of Communion

from *Come Away My Beloved*

Pray to thy Father which is in secret; and thy Father
which seeth in secret shall reward thee openly.

MATTHEW 6:6

My beloved, My heart longs after you. Do not grieve Me by
your indifference. I would gather you, but you do not heed Me.
I would embrace and caress you, but you are impatient to be
on your way. You cannot please Me thus.

I have called you to come into the secret chambers of solitary
communion. They are dark, but the comfort of My Person is
there. Out of darkness comes great treasure.

The dazzle and glitter of public life is attractive to the natural eye, but I would closet you in the secret places of humility
and discipline of soul, denying the things that pertain to the
outward man in order to perfect the inner life and enrich your
knowledge of Myself.

What has God shown me in His secret chamber?

Take No Thought for Tomorrow

from *Progress of Another Pilgrim*

Consider the lilies of the field. . .they toil not,
neither do they spin: And yet. . .even Solomon in
all his glory was not arrayed like one of these.

MATTHEW 6:28-29

***

*M*y children are never more well cared for than when they commit their earthly needs to Me. I am not a pauper, neither will I let you be financially embarrassed; let go your earthly cares.

I do not forbid you to work, only to worry. The best way to break the power of worry is to refuse to take thought for tomorrow. Today is rarely a problem. Most anxious thoughts are related to the future. Put all of tomorrow into My keeping.

For today you need Wisdom. For tomorrow you need Faith. Try it, and you will never want to go back to the old way.

Worry or faith—which do I have?

Resignation

from *Come Away My Beloved*

Seek ye first the kingdom of God and His righteousness;
and all these things shall be added unto you.

MATTHEW 6:33

*I*ncline your heart to Me, and attune your ear to My voice.
For I have an urgent message to give you.

Do not set out to establish your own designs. I have already set in motion My divine will and purpose, and I would not have you interfere. I am jealous of My children: they are Mine, and you shall not intrude in any way to hinder My plans from working out. Yes, you may do many things, but only that which I direct you to do can have My blessing.

Resign all into My hands—your loved ones as well as your own self. Be obedient to the still, small voice. Fret not about carnal things, but concern yourself first and always with spiritual values.

What am I seeking first?

One Day at a Time

from *Come Away My Beloved*

Therefore do not worry about tomorrow,
for tomorrow will worry about its own things.
Sufficient for the day is its own trouble.

MATTHEW 6:34 NKJV

My child, have you not known the way of the Lord, and can you not trust Him now? Nothing shall befall you but that which comes from His hand. No one shall set upon you to hurt you, for your God has built around you a wall of fire.

Be content with what each day brings, rejoicing in your God, for surely He shall deliver you. He is the One who has brought you here.

His way is discernable to the eye of faith. His heart is surely your strong tower. In His affection you have security. In His love are your hope and your peace.

How content am I with what each day brings?

The Road Is Steep

from *Come Away My Beloved*

Narrow is the gate and difficult is the way which
leads to life, and there are few who find it.

MATTHEW 7:14 NKJV

---

*Y*ou are a chosen vessel to Me, so do not be filled with filthy
lucre. Be undefiled by the lusts of the flesh and untarnished
by the pride of life. Be wholesome, humble, simple; for simplicity and a spirit of humility befit one who serves the Lord.

Pride lifts up. It exalts self rather than Christ. Humility
brings down to the level of service, and you are not to be wor-
shiped, but to serve.

You are My treasure. I delight in you when you are fully
yielded to Me with no thoughts of personal ambition or
achievement. If you wish for anything, wish for more of My
nearness. If you long after anything, long after more of My
righteousness and more of My love.

Am I wholesome, humble, and simple—or prideful?

Break Old Patterns

from *Progress of Another Pilgrim*

But Jesus said unto him, Follow me;
and let the dead bury their dead.

MATTHEW 8:22

---

*T*he time is now because the hour is late; yes, there is not a day left, but an hour. There is not time for incidentals because of the sheer urgency. Run after Me as I move, because I am moving rapidly and am doing a quick work. Pay no attention to any voice except the voice of the Spirit. Let no one use you except the Father. Believe no one except the Son. Live in expectancy and move in absolute obedience.

Break out of old patterns, and make no provision for your own personal wishes. Purify your desires so that you do not stand in your own way.

Am I running after Jesus or the world?

Faith and Action

from *Come Away My Beloved*

According to your faith be it unto you.

MATTHEW 9:29

---

*M*y promises are of no avail to you except as you apply and appropriate them by faith. In your daily walk, you shall be victorious only to the degree that you trust Me. I can help you only as you ask. I will meet you at every point where you put action alongside your prayers.

Overburdened as the world is with trouble and sickness, I need those who have proved My sufficiency in personal experience to lead the suffering to the fountains of life.

Never begrudge time given to chronic complainers, but recognize in each encounter the opportunity to speak a word that may lead to their liberation. No case is too hard for Me.

How has my life proved Jesus' sufficiency?

I Am Everywhere

from *Progress of Another Pilgrim*

Heal the sick, cleanse the lepers, raise the dead,
cast out devils: freely ye have received, freely give.

MATTHEW 10:8

*N*ever flounder on the rocks of indecision. The call of My
heart to you is for your utter abandon to the waters of My will.
I am everywhere. Think not that any man can shut Me out.
Wherever you go you bear the Wind of the Spirit. It shall bring
new life into any situation. It shall breathe upon the dead, and
they shall live. It shall touch the one who has completely given
up with a ray of new courage, so that though he may have lost
all hope he shall be lifted out of the place of despondency into
My loving arms and into an atmosphere of faith once again.

How is the "Wind of the Spirit" working through me?

Thy God Forever

from *Dialogues with God*

But the very hairs of your head are all numbered.

MATTHEW 10:30

*B*ehold, I am Thy God forever. I am with thee. In the time of trouble, I will be thy strong defense, and in the hour of need, I am thy sure habitation.

Mine eye is ever watchful and I shall undertake for thee according to My glorious riches. Is it not written: "The very hairs of your head are all numbered" (Matthew 10:30)? Surely My love for thee is altered by no external circumstances.

I am the Lord thy God that changeth not, neither grows weary nor irritable. My love is constant. Hold to this one thing as the needle holds to the pole.

I shall not disappoint thee in any way.

Am I holding fast to God alone?

The Spiritual Realm

from *On the Highroad of Surrender*

Come to Me, all you who labor and are heavy laden,
and I will give you rest. Take My yoke upon you
and learn from Me, for I am gentle and lowly in heart,
and you will find rest for your souls.

MATTHEW 11:28-29 NKJV

𝒟o not be concerned about failing people. Your only true concern should be that you not fail Me. I am making last-minute preparations for My soon-coming. The table is already spread for the marriage supper for the Lamb. Do not frustrate My plans for you by pursuing your own.

I want you walking and expressing in the spiritual realm. For this purpose have I painstakingly prepared your soul. Cast aside your carnal reasoning. Cast aside even your consideration for people and the threat of disappointing them. Would you rather that I be disappointed, in preference to others? Can you not trust Me? Would I fail anyone?

Who am I most concerned about serving?

Release Your Grief

Take My yoke upon you and learn from Me,
for I am gentle and lowly in heart,
and you will find rest for your souls.

MATTHEW 11:29 NKJV

*M*y child, lean your head upon My bosom. I know well your weariness, and every burden I would lift. Never bury your griefs, but offer them up to Me. You will relieve your soul of much strain if you can lay every care in My hand. Never cling to any trouble, hoping to resolve it yourself, but turn it over to Me. In doing so, you will free Me to work it out.

*What personal grief can I place
in Jesus' hands?*

Avoid Frivolity

from *Progress of Another Pilgrim*

But I say unto you, That every idle word
that men shall speak, they shall give account
thereof in the day of judgment.

MATTHEW 12:36

Avoid frivolity with the same carefulness as you disdain the grosser sins. The latter are transgressions of the law of God, but the former is a thief and will rob both yourself and others of spiritual good.

A bantering spirit may cause you to be oblivious to opportunities to minister that may lie directly in your path. Thus if you are indulging in spiritual profligacy, you rob the other person of the blessing you could have given, and you rob yourself of the reward you would have received had you been walking softly in the Spirit.

What must I do to avoid frivolity?

Guard Against Foolishness

from *Progress of Another Pilgrim*

For by thy words thou shalt be justified,
and by thy words thou shalt be condemned.

MATTHEW 12:37

*Y*ou may have My joy in abundance, but guard your own spirit against foolishness. Thoughts of nonsense and empty words are utter waste. I can use them in no way at all.

All words are either actively good or actively negative, and if they are negative, they are destructive. They will nullify the testimony I would establish when you speak My words, so that if you mix the two, the good will be cancelled out by the evil.

You cannot afford such carelessness. My servants must be wise as serpents and blameless as doves. Let your every word be full of grace and taste of the saltiness of divine goodness. Let it be known of you by your good conversation that you have been much with Me.

What guards against foolishness can I establish?

On Coping with Success

from *On the Highroad of Surrender*

Because it has been given to you to know the mysteries of
the kingdom of heaven, but to them it has not been given.
For whoever has, to him more will be given, and he will
have abundance; but whoever does not have, even what
he has will be taken away from him.

MATTHEW 13:11-12 NKJV

*B*e never entangled by thoughts concerning the reactions
of others to your ministry. No decision should ever be made on
this basis. Minister, and follow the leading of the Spirit. Search
your heart, and pray for the strength to receive great results.

I may withhold blessings because in My love and wisdom I
foresee your own unreadiness to receive. Learn how to prepare
your mind and heart to cope with success; otherwise, when it
comes you may by your very unreadiness and lack of fortitude
undo the good that has been done.

How concerned am I about other people's approval?

Angels Are Separating

from *Progress of Another Pilgrim*

The harvest is the end of the world;
and the reapers are the angels.

MATTHEW 13:39

⸰⸱⸰⸱⸰

*H*ave I not spoken concerning the future day, that it shall
be a day of the gathering of the wheat and of the destruction
of the tares? Have I not said this work shall be done by angels?

You have been aware of the presence and ministry of
angels. You, as believers, are being gathered unto the Father.
Meanwhile the children of wrath and disobedience are being
separated and gathered to each other.

Truly, angels are separating. Know this when you would
wonder why one is brought in and another goes out into the
night, never to return. Question it not, for you are seeing this
prophecy fulfilled, at least in part. It shall be accelerated as
the end draws nearer.

You shall find in this understanding much peace of heart.

What is my part in the harvest?

Faith Released

from *On the Highroad of Surrender*

For whoever desires to save his life will lose it,
and whoever loses his life for My sake will find it.

MATTHEW 16:25 NKJV

---

*L*ean hard on Me, My child, and I will be your peace. Storms shall not disquiet the trusting heart, but songs of praise and victory shall spring from the place of testing, and mercy shall prevail where faith is released, in spite of every contrary wind.

No harm can come to the one who looks to Me as his protection, but he who endeavors to protect himself shall be exposed to the destructive forces he seeks to escape.

He shall not know peace who runs after the rewards of the world.

Where do I turn for protection?

Outflow

from *On the Highroad of Surrender*

For what is a man profited if he gains the whole world,
and loses his own soul? Or what will a man
give in exchange for his soul?

MATTHEW 16:26 NKJV

*B*lessings are released when the soul is content with nothing of earthly value. The spirit is prepared for worldly success only after it has learned to care nothing for it. I fill the hand that lies open in worship. The hand that grasps shall be forever empty.

Learn to leave to My love and wisdom all your destiny. Nothing ought concern you but the health of your soul and the outflow of your life. You will free your soul as you refuse to seek anything and desire only to give. Then shall I bless you with increase and only then will it not impoverish your spirit.

How is the outflow of my life?

Challenge and Growth

from *On the Highroad of Surrender*

This kind does not go out except
by prayer and fasting.

MATTHEW 17:21 NKJV

———◦◦———◦◦———◦◦———

*I*n all the challenges of life, My hand is outstretched to give
you courage. No stress need overwhelm if your confidence is
in Me. To lean upon the arm of flesh brings certain disaster.

When the psalmist penned, "From the Lord comes my help,"
he excluded all other sources. Effective faith is born of total
consecration. My Spirit alone can bring forth this kind of
dedication and inner strength.

Continual challenges bring constant growth, and when you
pray for respite from the conflict, you rob your soul and retard
its maturation.

Hold before Me at all times a heart that prefers instruction
to comfort. You cannot have both.

Do I prefer instruction to comfort?

God's Purpose

from *On the Highroad of Surrender*

Now behold, one came and said to Him, "Good Teacher,
what good thing shall I do that I may have eternal life?"
So He said to him, "Why do you call Me good? No one is good
but One, that is, God. But if you want to enter into life,
keep the commandments."

MATTHEW 19:16-17 NKJV

God's purpose in making you holy involves His own glory.
He is not waiting to hear you called holy; He is listening to
hear you call Him holy. He is not interested in making you a
reputation, but in making you a disciple.

The rich young ruler flattered Jesus by addressing him as
"good master," and Jesus rebuked him, pressing upon him the
necessity to decide either to not call him good, or to acknowl-
edge His deity. How then can He be pleased that one should
desire such a reputation?

Am I truly Jesus' disciple?

Love's Servant

from *Make Haste My Beloved*

He that is greatest among you shall be your servant.

MATTHEW 23:11

You seek acceptance, forgetting that Jesus was despised and rejected.

You seek happiness, ignoring the fact that He was a man of sorrows.

You seek security, when the Son of Man had no certain place to lay His head.

Why do you seek falsely? Because you have not learned to love. Love changes all the desires. Love knows that doing the Father's will is the only thing of value. Because love does not seek its own, it is not dismayed when circumstances are unfavorable.

He who has love will labor happily though unremunerated and sacrifice personal comfort without protest or complaint. He will measure happiness by his power to give and weakness by his limitation to bring comfort to those in need.

Love is the source of joy, the touchstone of all meaningful human expression.

How well do I love when circumstances are unfavorable?

The Echo of My Voice

from *On the Highroad of Surrender*

Woe to you, scribes and Pharisees, hypocrites!
For you cleanse the outside of the cup and dish, but inside
they are full of extortion and self-indulgence.

MATTHEW 23:25 NKJV

*O*My child, the cry of your soul is the echo of My voice calling you to repentance. Your love for Me will place you under
My chastening rod, for as long as you love Me, you will seek
My face even when you anticipate My reproach. The hand of
punishment that restores to fellowship is kinder than the
hand of sympathy of the one who would palliate your con-
science in an evil action.

Let Me deal with any unsoundness in your spirit, and I will
spare you the humiliation of open shame. Inner conviction
comes through My Word, and this is your only sure way of
finding peace in My presence.

When have I felt God's conviction concerning my deeds?

Responsibilities and Privileges

from Progress of Another Pilgrim

For unto every one that hath shall be given,
and he shall have abundance: but from him that hath
not shall be taken away even that which he hath.

MATTHEW 25:29

*R*esponsibilities always increase in proportion to privileges. He who is recipient of great spiritual riches, of him will I require much in the way of ministry. Let the earthly life of the Lord Jesus be an example to you. Day and night He toiled, praying by night and working by day. So must you. The present hour is even more critical because the time of final judgment is coming upon mankind. Darkness is deepening, and the light of My witness is more needed than ever before.

Be faithful, and you shall deliver others and preserve your own soul.

What responsibilities and privileges has God given me?

The Broadening View

from *Dialogues with God*

For there is nothing hid, which shall not be manifested;
neither was any thing kept secret,
but that it should come abroad.

MARK 4:22

⸺•⸺ ⸺•⸺ ⸺•⸺

I have many glorious facets of truth to reveal to thee, but ye are not able to receive them all at once. Whatever truths may be obscure to thee now, I am anxiously waiting to make plain.

So give thyself to diligent study—yea, search the scriptures for they are given for the purpose of revealing Me. It shall be as when one ascends a mountain, and from each successively higher vantage point he thrills at an increasingly broadening view. I will take thee progressively higher via the written Word until that day when ye shall see Me face to face! Then shall ye know Me and understand Me even as I now know you.

What view am I seeing?

The Listening Ear

from On the Highroad of Surrender

If any man have ears to hear, let him hear.
And he said unto them, Take heed what ye hear:
with what measure ye mete, it shall be measured to you:
and unto you that hear shall more be given.

MARK 4:23-24

I will make My message very clear to the honest heart. You would be furthered more in your spiritual life if you spent more time praying that duplicity be eradicated from your heart than by praying to have more truth revealed to you. In most cases, you already have knowledge of more truth than you are practicing. To seek further truth before surrendering to the light already received is to invite destruction.

My commandments are very precious to those who are desirous of doing My will. Those who truly wish to please Me do not seek ways to rationalize and bypass My laws.

How does my knowledge compare with my practice?

Dismiss with Dispatch

from *Progress of Another Pilgrim*

And when he was come into the ship, he that had
been possessed with the devil prayed him that he might
be with him. Howbeit Jesus suffered him not,
but saith unto him, Go home to thy friends,
and tell them how great things the Lord hath done for thee.

MARK 5:18-19

*N*othing I am doing would seem strange to you if you had
been more attentive to My voice.

I can lead you only as you wait upon Me for guidance. Man
will always take you down the wrong path. It is folly to stumble along in blindness. I am your friend. Can you not trust My
love? Would I ever harm you? Do I not give you a full measure
of joy?

Do I view Jesus as my friend?

Inner Communion

from *Progress of Another Pilgrim*

And whosoever shall not receive you, nor hear you,
when ye depart thence, shake off the dust under
your feet for a testimony against them.

MARK 6:11

*B*ow before Me in adoration and humility and you need not stoop before any man. Know that when I place upon your ministry the seal of Mine approval it shall no longer be important to you whether or not you are accepted by any other.

This is an activity in which we are co-laborers together—I and you and the Father. Keep a strong awareness of this identification. You will lose the anointing if you allow anyone to enter and distract.

Stay in the holy place of inner communion and I will break forth through your vessel and manifest My glory outwardly.

How is my communion with God?

Be My Ally

from *Come Away My Beloved*

And he [Jesus] said unto them,
Come ye yourselves apart into a desert place,
and rest a while.

MARK 6:31

*M*y children, do not fear nor resist My voice. When I speak to you, you will know that it is I, the Lord God. As I spoke to Isaiah I will speak to you. Is it not strange that you are astonished at the way I speak to you? Instead, those who do not hear My voice ought to marvel!

Your busyness wearies Me. Small wonder you are yourself fatigued! Your fretfulness grieves Me. I long to take it from you and give you instead the balm of Gilead. Be My ally. I will endow you with life so dynamic that you will serve Me before you have time to even think about putting forth the effort to do so.

In what areas of my life do I need His balm today?

Sacrifice, My Status Symbol

from *Come Away My Beloved*

For whoever desires to save his life will lose it, but whoever
loses his life for My sake and the gospel's will save it.

MARK 8:35 NKJV

O wicked and perverse generation, have I been so long in
your midst and yet you have perceived Me not? Yes, and when
I speak to you, you do not hear.

O My children, you behave not as sons and daughters but
as strangers. You hold meetings in My Name, and give honor
to men, but not to Me. You boast that you serve Me, but in
truth you serve your own ego.

You would make Christianity pleasant and acceptable. Your
Savior did not find it so. You would make it comfortable and
accommodating to your own schedule. He knew nothing of
such a false religion.

Do you desire to truly follow Me? Look for the bloodstained
prints of My feet.

Who am I really serving today?

Key to Joy

from *On the Highroad of Surrender*

For whoever desires to save his life will lose it,
but whoever loses his life for My sake and the gospel's
will save it. For what will it profit a man if he gains
the whole world, and loses his own soul?

MARK 8:35-36 NKJV

*S*urrender is the key to joy. By release the soul is freed.
Bondage is the twin of selfishness. To hold is to lose, and to
free is to gain.

Meditation opens the door to revelation, and revelation
brings liberation. Test it in any given situation. You will find
that you hold in your own hand the instrument of life. It will
work like a magic eye to open the heaviest door.

Am I in bondage, or have I surrendered?

By Silence Ye Rob Me of My Glory

from *Dialogues with God*

Whosoever therefore shall be ashamed of me and
of my words in this adulterous and sinful generation;
of him also shall the Son of man be ashamed, when he
cometh in the glory of his Father with the holy angels.

MARK 8:38

*Y*ea, My child, I have been betrayed more times by silence
than by words. By words a man may sin against Me, but by
silence do ye rob Me of My Glory.

Never miss an opportunity to uphold Me; and know this: as
ye testify of Me and plead My cause before men, I will surely
plead thy cause and witness for thee before the Father.

But as it is written: if you are ashamed of Me before men, I
will be ashamed of you when I stand before the Father in your
behalf (Mark 8:38).

How have I robbed God of His glory?

Perspective and Depth

from *Progress of Another Pilgrim*

And Peter answered and said to Jesus, Master,
it is good for us to be here: and let us make three tabernacles;
one for thee, and one for Moses, and one for Elias. For he wist
not what to say; for they were sore afraid.

MARK 9:5-6

---

*Y*ou need perspective and depth. This never comes from
public converse, but from private communion. You seek to
learn from others, but I long to tell you things I may never be
able to tell them. I say this not to tempt you to feel proud, but
to explain to you that I do not share the same truths with all.
There are truths I wish to give you. You may never be asked to
share them with any other person. They may be just for you—
or they may be for people you have never seen as yet.

What private truths has God shown me?

Faith Reaches Beyond

from *On the Highroad of Surrender*

Whatever things you ask when you pray, believe that
you receive them, and you will have them.

MARK 11:24 NKJV

---

*F*aith, My child, reaches out beyond the need and into the supply. Always remember that the supply is greater than the need.

Do you need forgiveness? Lo, I have provided enough that if
all human souls ever created turned to Me in repentance, they
would be fully pardoned. Will I then deem your sins too great
for remission?

Do you need power to overcome temptation? Lo, I have overcome, and in Me there is victory for every soul that casts itself
upon My mercy.

It is patience for which you pray? Know that in the Spirit
there is no time, and that for which you wait is already given
and only waits your receiving.

Do I trust God to supply all my needs?

The Divine Commission

from *Come Away My Beloved*

And He said to them, "Go into all the world,
and preach the gospel to every creature."

MARK 16:15 NJKV

My child, do not chafe at the bit. It is I who have put it in your mouth. You question My direction because it is not the common way. But I would have you take a path that is quite different from the paths of your friends, and it is because I would bring you into a place in Me and a ministry in which they have no part.

Do not hesitate, and do not falter. In this hour you should be gripped with one consuming purpose—to find the place I have for you.

Your heart will grow cold unless you keep it close to Mine. Your love shall be turned to indifference unless you keep the cross before your eyes.

Have I found God's place for me?

Exercise Your Faith

from *Progress of Another Pilgrim*

And they went forth, and preached every where,
the Lord working with them, and confirming
the word with signs following. Amen.

MARK 16:20

*Y*ou are bound by pride and self-satisfaction. I am not pleased. I need your witness in a free flow. You must be more articulate. Exercise your faith, knowing that I will give you the right words and will fill them with the power of My Spirit, and they shall be used by Me to bring salvation and deliverance.

Be not detained by self-doubt. Rely on Me, and do not regard your own limitations as a liability.

I will manifest through you in a mighty way if you will only give Me the opportunity. Be My mouthpiece, and I will supply the words and the message.

Am I relying on God or focused on my limitations?

A Door of Utterance

from *Progress of Another Pilgrim*

And they went forth, and preached every where,
the Lord working with them, and confirming
the word with signs following. Amen.

MARK 16:20

*B*ehold, I set before you a door of utterance. You shall open your mouth, and I will fill it. You shall go and not be detained. You shall glorify Me, and your own vessel shall be an open channel for the river of My grace.

You shall bring healing. You shall bring hope. I shall endue you with power from on high, and I shall magnify My word so that as you speak it forth I will confirm it, even with miracles following. Be faithful, and deliver My word, and I will surely bless it and cause it to be a creative word, a life-giving word, yes, a word of deliverance.

What words has God put into my mouth?

Call of the Turtledove

from *Come Away My Beloved*

When Elizabeth heard the greeting of Mary. . . the babe leaped
in her womb; and Elizabeth was filled with the Holy Spirit.

LUKE 1:41 NKJV

*O*My children, there is the sound of the turtledove echoing
throughout the land. It is the voice of the Bridegroom calling
His Bride. It is the call of love, and those who truly love Him
will respond.

Like attracts like, and love has always been the test of true
discipleship. Those listening to the voice of their Beloved
will not be deafened by the cries of men. In a world filled with
noises, they will hear Him.

Yes, they shall even hear the tender cooing of the turtledove!
Like Elizabeth when she was greeted by Mary, the response was
an inner, involuntary response to the nearness of the Christ.

Anticipate Me. Watch for Me. Your heart will listen, and
your heart shall hear.

What has my heart heard from God?

Love Endures

from *On the Highroad of Surrender*

He has filled the hungry with good things,
And the rich He has sent away empty.

LUKE 1:53 NKJV

*T*hrough many bewildering experiences I deal with the soul. When there is submission of spirit, all things work together for good.

The soul that submits to My disciplines loves Me. Love will hold you steady beneath the chastening rod because love believes and hopes in all things (1 Corinthians 13:7). Love will never fail. It will endure whatever comes because it rests in Me rather than in the circumstance.

You need never be deprived of comfort as long as your desires are fulfilled in Me; for I satisfy the hungry with good things, while the rich go empty away (Luke 1:53). He who goes away will always be empty in spite of his riches. He who seeks Me will never be unhappy or poor.

Is my spirit submitted to Him?

I Control the Winds

from *Come Away My Beloved*

Guide our feet into the way of peace.

LUKE 1:79

---

*M*y child, do not be dismayed by any calamity that befalls you. Your times are in My hand. Never doubt My care. Never question My dealings. I am leading you by the narrowness of the way. It is often a difficult and precipitous path, but I would assure you of My hand of protection.

Put your life in My hands, and it will be for you a place of peace and of spiritual comfort. So long as you abide in this place, I will control the rains that fall upon you and the winds that blow. So long as you are in My hands, you are in a garrison the walls of which no enemy will scale.

Have I put my life fully in His hands?

Be Deaf to the Cry of the Crowd

from *On the Highroad of Surrender*

Then passing through the midst of them, He went His way.

LUKE 4:30 NKJV

Ah, My child, this is the secret! Always there will be those who are crowding the way. They will seem to cover the path. If you give power to their words and actions, they will encompass you and prevent your moving ahead. Go your way.

The moment you set your spiritual eye upon the goal I have given you, the bondage of people is broken. You will be able, as Jesus was, to pass through the midst of them and be freed to be about your Father's business. Do not allow yourself to be trapped by the multitude. Your own higher vision will free you, and there is a path in the Spirit, if you walk in it, where there is free motion.

How much have I let the crowd affect my spiritual walk?

The Gift of Forgiveness

from *Come Away My Beloved*

Launch out into the deep and let down your nets for a catch.

LUKE 5:4 NJKV

*O*My child, come to Me—I want to give you a new gift. I want you to see all people as being under the shed sacrifice of the blood of Christ.

He has died for all. His forgiveness encompasses all. Tell them the Good News. It is the confidence in your own heart that will engender faith to receive within the hearts of others.

Freely forgive all, as you have freely loved all. Those to whom you extend My forgiveness will come to experience it for themselves. It is like extending a helping hand to lift another across a brook. Having gained the safety of the other side, he needs your help no longer but stands as secure as yourself; but he needed assistance in crossing over.

Who can I share Jesus with today?

Mercy

from *On the Highroad of Surrender*

But love your enemies, do good, and lend, hoping for nothing
in return; and your reward will be great, and you will be sons
of the Highest. For He is kind to the unthankful and evil.
Therefore be merciful, just as your Father also is merciful.

LUKE 6:35-36 NKJV

*M*ercy is the extension of My grace. Whenever you show
mercy to another, you express My love. I rejoice in forgiveness. I do not give grudgingly. You have been told to give
cheerfully of your substance; now I say unto you, do the same
in the Spirit. When you are called upon to be tolerant—to
forgive—do not question and do not delay.

Deal justly, but in patience and understanding, and add
not evil upon evil. As I have given to you, so likewise do you
to others; otherwise, you violate My mercy as it would flow
through you.

Who should I show mercy to today?

The Economy of the Kingdom

from *Come Away My Beloved*

For with the same measure that you use,
it will be measured back to you.

LUKE 6:38 NKJV

---

*B*ring Me all the tithes, and I will open the gates of heaven and pour down upon you a fourfold blessing. Yes, I will bless you in the grace of giving, and I will bless you with joy. You shall open the door of ministry for My servants, and you shall partake of the fruits that will come as a result.

You will never give to Me and become the poorer for it. In exchange for your small gifts, you shall be given My boundless riches. Through the contribution that comes from a willing heart, I will be freed to bestow the abundance of heaven, treasures you could never purchase from the world.

With what measure am I giving?

Humbled Hearts

from *Come Away My Beloved*

How can you say. . ."Brother, let me remove the speck
that is in your eye," when you yourself do not
see the plank that is in your own eye?

LUKE 6:42 NKJV

———

My people, I have called you to repentance and confession
and forgiveness and cleansing, but you have listened to My
words as though they were of little consequence. Behold, I say:
You cannot resist My Spirit without suffering pain, and you
cannot turn a deaf ear to My words without falling into the
snare of the enemy.

Look no more to My hand to supply freely your needs when
you have not cleansed your hands and come to Me with a broken and a contrite heart. You need not expect Me to speak to
you when your ears are heavy from listening to evil reports.

How humble is my heart?

On Doing the Father's Work

from *Come Away My Beloved*

Every tree is known by its own fruit.
For men do not gather figs from thorns,
nor do they gather grapes from a bramble bush.

LUKE 6:44 NKJV

*B*ehold, there is a day coming when you will regret your lethargy, and you will ask, "Why did we leave the vineyard of the Lord untended?" Those things that have occupied you will appear for what they are—chaff and worthlessness. For there will be nothing of lasting value, and no reward for the works of your hands which you have done in your own strength, and which I have not commanded you to do.

I have fashioned you for better things. Do not fail Me. Place your life under My divine control and learn to live in the full blessing of My highest will.

I will strengthen you and comfort you; I will lead you by the hand.

Is my life under God's control?

Seers

from *On the Highroad of Surrender*

Therefore take heed how you hear. For whoever has,
to him more will be given; and whoever does not have,
even what he seems to have will be taken from him.

LUKE 8:18 NKJV

*T*here is a spirit of bewilderment abroad in the land today
that causes people to go about as though they were moving
through a dense fog. Vision is obscured. Never have I needed
watchmen, heralds, prophets, and seers as I need them in this
hour.

Stay close to Me no matter what attractions exert themselves to draw you away. I need more time with you, and you
need to give fuller attention to the things of the Spirit.

You can never fail to hear My voice if your ears have been
unstopped by obedience and the desire to please and serve Me.

What do I need to do to hear God's voice?

A Fresh Move of Faith

from On the Highroad of Surrender

No one, having put his hand to the plow,
and looking back, is fit for the kingdom of God.

LUKE 9:62 NKJV

*B*elieve Me for new things. Venture forth in trust. It is time
to thrust forward in a new spearhead, a fresh move of faith.
Fight procrastination as you would resist evil, for surely it is
the enemy of good.

Put forth your hand to the plow and look not back, neither
count the cost. I will repay you in the currency of eternity.
Keep your eyes on Me and walk humbly. You are not to doctor
the souls of others, but introduce them to the Great Physician
and provide a spiritually healthy atmosphere for those who
seek help.

In what ways do I procrastinate?

Disappointment

from *On the Highroad of Surrender*

No one, having put his hand to the plow,
and looking back, is fit for the kingdom of God.

LUKE 9:62 NKJV

---

*O*ut of every disappointment there is to be gleaned some treasure. The enemy would whisper "all is lost." I say to you, much can be gained.

Refuse the temptation to brood over what is gone. It has passed into the area of My sovereignty. The present challenge requires your undivided attention.

Give no time to dark thoughts. Depression undermines the vigor of the soul.

How do I respond to disappointment?

An Anointed Tongue

from *Progress of Another Pilgrim*

After these things the Lord appointed other seventy also,
and sent them two and two before his face into every city
and place, whither he himself would come.

LUKE 10:1

I have called you to a special ministry, and it cannot be carried out properly without My full blessing.

Let Me anoint your tongue, and you shall speak with
divine authority and never again will you say, "I am a weak
and inadequate vessel." I shall put words into your heart and
speak them forth from your lips, and hearts shall burn as the
message goes out.

You shall know that it is My message and My words that
are spoken. The fruits you shall offer up to Me, for you shall
know truly that it is the Lord your God who has brought to
pass His own word of promise.

What kind of speech comes off my tongue?

Speak the Word of Faith

from *On the Highroad of Surrender*

The harvest truly is great, but the laborers are few;
therefore pray the Lord of the harvest to send
out laborers into His harvest.

LUKE 10:2 NKJV

*L*earn to speak the word of faith and the word of knowledge as I put it in your mouth. Doors will be opened in this simple fashion, and entrance given to hearts that would otherwise have remained closed to the gospel. Once the door is open, you may plant the seed of faith and it will spring forth into eternal life.

Go not to those who are dull of hearing, for their deafness will only increase. Go to the tender, the needy, the broken-hearted, and the suffering. I shall minister in love and compassion, and I shall use you as My mouthpiece.

Do I speak as God commands?

Closed Doors

from *On the Highroad of Surrender*

Behold, I give you the authority to trample on serpents
and scorpions, and over all the power of the enemy,
and nothing shall by any means hurt you.

LUKE 10:19 NKJV

*N*ever lose heart when confronted by disappointment.
Remember always that I control all that touches you, and
as I move to order your life, I not only open the right doors,
but close the wrong ones. Whenever a wrong door is closed, it
is by My hand as much as when a right one opens. In this way
I not only bring you joy but spare you pain. Trust Me.

Have I not said that nothing shall harm you?

What doors has God opened and closed in my life?

The Soul Is Directional

from *Progress of Another Pilgrim*

And Jesus answered and said unto her, Martha, Martha,
thou art careful and troubled about many things:
But one thing is needful: and Mary hath chosen that
good part, which shall not be taken away from her.

LUKE 10:41-42

*M*y people need direction. There are many pressures
which influence them, but they need to hear a clear voice
giving them the wisdom of God.

The soul is directional, and any heart turned toward Me in
an attitude of true worship shall receive from Me a quickening flow of life. It cannot be otherwise.

Those who do not hear Me are occupying themselves with
other thoughts. They may even be studying the Bible and fail to
hear My voice, but they cannot worship Me and miss Me.

What direction is my soul headed in?

Inattention

from *On the Highroad of Surrender*

Therefore take heed that the light which is in you is not
darkness. If then your whole body is full of light, having no
part dark, the whole body will be full of light, as when the
bright shining of a lamp gives you light.

LUKE 11:35-36 NKJV

—•✛•——•✛•——•✛•—

*I*f you will listen to My voice, I will reveal Myself. I am gracious and patient, but I am grieved by your hardness of heart
and inattention. Open rebellion usually brings immediate
punishment. Inattention can be even more destructive to the
soul, because it often goes unnoticed and unrepented, and is a
secret, unexposed sin.

Cast it out in Jesus' Name, and refuse the robber who
would take your dearest treasure. . .your singleness of heart in
your love for Me.

How single-hearted am I?

No Fear

from *Come Away My Beloved*

Do not fear, little flock, for it is your Father's
good pleasure to give you the kingdom.
LUKE 12:32 NKJV

No, My children, do not fear. Remember the words of Holy
Scripture: "Do not fear, little flock, for it is your Father's good
pleasure to give you the kingdom" (Luke 12:32). Here you have
it again—I am not simply preserving you, but I am doing so
for the purpose of sharing with you My kingdom power. If you
can catch the vision of what the days ahead hold in store for
you in My great kingdom, you will gain a whole new perspective, so that as you view the present, transient scene, its true
dimension will come into focus in proportion to the whole
panoramic picture.

Am I getting God's picture of my life?

The Highroad of Absolute Surrender

from *On the Highroad of Surrender*

Do not fear, little flock, for it is your Father's
good pleasure to give you the kingdom.

LUKE 12:32 NKJV

---

*M*y little one, come close to Me. I have consolations for your soul that surpass your sharpest grief. I have walked through the deepest waters, and I am with you as you experience your baptism of sorrow. It is the path that leads to the gate of glory, and the Father waits to greet you there. It is not heaven of which I speak. It is a blessedness of spirit given to those who have passed through tribulations and have set their feet on the highroad of absolute surrender. From this place there is no turning back.

It may cost you all, but you cannot fathom what I have in store for you.

Hold fast to My hand.

Have I absolutely surrendered to God?

The Sense of Perspective

from *Come Away My Beloved*

Do not fear, little flock, for it is your Father's
good pleasure to give you the kingdom.

LUKE 12:32 NKJV

By design of man, out of the cruelty of wicked hearts,
Christ was made a martyr. But by the Hand of a greater power,
He was made to become a Savior—even the Savior of the very
men who put Him to death.

My children, do not fear. I am not simply preserving you,
but I am doing so for the purpose of sharing with you My
kingdom power.

How can I see my life from God's vantage point?

Be Much with Me

from *Come Away My Beloved*

Therefore you also be ready, for the Son of Man
is coming at an hour you do not expect.

LUKE 12:40 NKJV

*M*y people, set the watch in the nighttime; yes, rise and
pray, and do not let that hour come upon you unaware.

For the time is short; yes, the storm is gathering fast. Can
you not discern the events that are currently shaping up in
the affairs of men, and be as keen to observe their portent and
know that disaster and holocaust are in the making?

Be more with Me, and let My Spirit pervade your spirit,
and you shall be more influenced by Me than by the world
around you.

Be much with Me, for there is a great and heavy burden on
My heart.

How can I be often with Him?

I Shall Come Singing

from *Come Away My Beloved*

Be ready, for the Son of Man is coming
at an hour you do not expect.

LUKE 12:40 NKJV

*M*y children, be silent before Me. I will lift up My voice
as the sound of a trumpet—I will speak clearly to you, for the
hour is at hand.

Be obedient, and raise your standards of discipline and dedication to a higher level. For My face is set toward My imminent
return to earth. I wait only the release from the Father's hand.

Though I am ready and longing to come to you, you are
not yet ready. You have spurned My entreaties, and you have
fought against the restraints of the Spirit.

Keep your vision filled with Me. Keep your life in tune and
your worship in mutual harmony.

For I will come singing, and what will you be if you are in
discord?

Is my life in tune with God's will?

Harmony of Purpose

from *Progress of Another Pilgrim*

Whosoever. . .forsaketh not all that he hath,
he cannot be my disciple.

LUKE 14:33

If My people honor Me in their hearts, I will put My word upon their lips. Those who seek to live in obedience to My commandments will be brought into conformity with My nature, and these will I use to fulfill My purposes. Do not men do likewise? When a man chooses a workman, he takes into account not only his natural capabilities for the task, but also whether or not there is harmony of thought, purpose, character, and vision. If a man's heart is not in his work, his abilities will not be enough in themselves to make him a success.

Many are zealous and eager to serve in the Kingdom, but I cannot use them because their desires and goals are at cross-purposes with Mine.

What are my real desires and goals?

Simplicity of Spirit

from *Progress of Another Pilgrim*

Whosoever shall not receive the kingdom of God
as a little child shall in no wise enter therein.

LUKE 18:17

*B*y simplicity of spirit the soul is protected against forces of destruction. He who clings to My hand in childlike trust shall walk with joy in a path of safety. He who seeks to preserve his own soul by the devices of his own intellect will be snared and brought into confusion and bondage.

The soul progresses by praise, worship, and love, but it is hindered by conscious thought and effort. Jesus taught this in His reference to the lilies of the field, how they neither toil nor spin, but are clothed by the Father.

Lay at My feet the anxiety about your own spiritual life, and give yourself to love Me and to worship Me. The results in your soul will be joy and victory.

Is my spirit simple or anxious?

I Await Your Desire

from *Progress of Another Pilgrim*

Now when Jesus heard these things, he said unto him,
Yet lackest thou one thing: sell all that thou hast,
and distribute unto the poor, and thou shalt have
treasure in heaven: and come, follow me.

LUKE 18:22

My child, truly I rejoice in ministering to an open heart.
I have so much to give and so few truly desire to receive. My
soul is enlarged with grieving because My people are so callous of spirit and so hard of heart. I would give so much more
abundantly if they would but ask.

I await your desire, because if I gave to you when your desire was small, you would not be prepared for receiving.

Hide nothing from Me. Bring Me everything, and repent of
anything you cannot offer Me as a holy gift. I would sanctify
your entire life. Release all to Me.

Have I released all to Him?

A Crucial Hour

from *Progress of Another Pilgrim*

Watch ye therefore, and pray always, that ye may be
accounted worthy to escape all these things that shall
come to pass, and to stand before the Son of man.

LUKE 21:36

*W*atch for the signs of My soon-coming. Do not be blind to
that which is transpiring around you and in the world. It has
been revealed to you what you may expect. No concern lies
more heavily on My heart than the preparation of My chosen
ones for the ingathering. I do not want My coming to be so
and catch you by surprise. Not only do you need to prepare
your own hearts, but I would use you to warn and help others.

This is no time for apathy. There has been no more crucial
hour in all man's history.

How prepared is my heart for the Lord's coming?

Anticipation, Meditation, Participation

from *On the Highroad of Surrender*

And in the daytime He was teaching in the temple,
but at night He went out and stayed on the mountain called
Olivet. Then early in the morning all the people came
to Him in the temple to hear Him.

LUKE 21:37-38 NKJV

———————

As you have honored Me with your lips, honor Me now with your ministry. Move on into active participation in My Will. Anticipation, meditation, and participation: there is a place for each of these as you move from one to the other.

Never get bogged down at any one of these points. Solitude and then service, and vice-versa. Neither is complete in itself. Each is enriched by the other. In solitude I minister to you, and in service I minister through you to others. Both are essential to your growth, and others are robbed of blessing if you hoard the riches of God and fail to share.

How much time do I make for solitude before God?

The Rod and the Look

from *On the Highroad of Surrender*

Peter remembered the word of the Lord, how He
had said to him, "Before the rooster crows, you will deny
Me three times." Then Peter went out and wept bitterly.

LUKE 22:61-62 NKJV

*T*he rod of punishment is laid upon the young child to correct and discipline him; but between two lovers, this is not the
method. I love you, and as you come into a closer relationship
with Me and the maturity of the walk of the true Bride, I deal
with you as a husband who gently remonstrates with his wife,
impressing upon her his thoughts and wishes, often with only
a look.

Just to draw near Me in a time of failure brings to the sensitive, loving spirit deeper suffering than was ever brought to a
disobedient child by the chastening rod.

Does God use a rod or a look with me?

Exalt His Name

from *Progress of Another Pilgrim*

In the beginning was the Word, and the Word
was with God, and the Word was God.
The same was in the beginning with God.

JOHN 1:1-2

*L*et none tell you My Son is as others. . .lo, He is the Son of God; yes, He is God the Son. Exalt His Name and rejoice in His majesty, for the heavens were fashioned by His hand, and man is His creation. What man of all earth's personages can lay claim to any such power of creation?

Yes, His works alone shall proclaim His power and deity. Man cannot extinguish the light of His glorious works.

What do I say when others deny Jesus is God?

The Cross in the Star

from *On the Highroad of Surrender*

The Word became flesh and dwelt among us,
and we beheld His glory, the glory as of the only
begotten of the Father, full of grace and truth.

JOHN 1:14 NKJV

The Cross, My child, is My symbol of Christmas. Wise men
followed the star, but it was the Savior whom they sought.
Wrapped that holy night in swaddling clothes was My perfect
gift to mankind. Cradled in the arms of Mary lay the only hope
of human salvation. Shepherds were drawn to worship Him by
the love that flowed through Him as He became the channel
for redeeming grace.

How have I praised God for His salvation through Jesus?

The Central Object

from *Progress of Another Pilgrim*

But whosoever drinketh of the water that I shall give him
shall never thirst; but the water that I shall give him shall be
in him a well of water springing up into everlasting life.

JOHN 4:14

*Y*ou shall hunger forever if you do not learn to feed on Me.
Your thirst shall never be quenched except you drink of the
Spirit and partake of the Christ life. No mortal shall bless you
thus.

Your heart shall rejoice when I am the central and highest
object of your affection. Dedication brings pure rapture when
the desire is wholly fixed upon Me! My Name alone, when
breathed in adoration, lifts the weariest heart from despair
and fills the seeking soul with exhilaration.

Is Jesus the central object of affection in my life?

You Shall Not Be Earthbound

from Come Away My Beloved

Whoever drinks of the water that I shall give him will never thirst. But the water that I shall give him will become in him a fountain of water springing up into everlasting life.

JOHN 4:14 NKJV

My children, what do you need today? I assure you, whatever you need, if you will look to Me, I will supply.

I will give you life, light, and strength. I will surround you and preserve you, so that in Me you may live, move, and have your being, existing in Me when apart from Me you would die.

You will live in a realm where the things of earth will not be able to limit your movement; but you will be freed in Me to a place where your spirit may soar as the eagle.

Does my spirit soar like an eagle?

Keep Your Channel Clear

from *Come Away My Beloved*

Whoever drinks of the water that I shall give him will never thirst. But the water that I shall give him will become in him a fountain of water springing up into everlasting life.

JOHN 4:14 NKJV

*O*My child, will I speak to you as one whose voice is lost in the noise of the crashing surf? Will you be like an instrument with broken strings from which the musician can bring forth no music?

No, I would have you be as the waterfall whose sound is continuous, as a great river whose flow is not interrupted. You shall not sing for a time and then be silent for a season. You shall not praise for a day and then revert to the current topics of everyday life.

Is my voice continuous in praise?

The Healing Pool

from *Progress of Another Pilgrim*

For an angel went down at a certain season into the pool,
and troubled the water: whosoever then first after the
troubling of the water stepped in was made whole of
whatsoever disease he had.

JOHN 5:4

*W*henever you are in any kind of trouble, know that My
Spirit in the midst is like the angel who stirred the Pool of
Bethesda and made it a place of healing. Disturbances which
give every appearance of being natural become infused with
divine purposes if your soul is allowed to lie in My hand.

You need not discern every experience in order to receive
a blessing. I Myself touch circumstances and add the power
of the miraculous, and you shall many times be startled to discover the reflection of My face in a very ordinary "pool."

Where have I seen the reflection of His face?

Mighty Triumph

from *Dialogues with God*

He that heareth my word, and believeth on him that sent
me, hath everlasting life, and shall not come into
condemnation; but is passed from death unto life.

JOHN 5:24

*T*he present conflict shall be counted trivial in the light
of the mighty triumph that is to come. For they shall stand
before Me—all the dead both small and great, to be judged: but
he that believeth in the Son hath everlasting life, and shall not
come into condemnation, but is passed already from death
into life. These who believe shall reign with Me, yea, they shall
judge both men and angels.

Hearken to My words in John 15 and simply abide in Me as
the branch in the vine. Make this present moment one of victory in Me, and live moment by moment, lost in My love.

How confident am I in God's mighty triumph?

The Apple of My Eye

from *Come Away My Beloved*

He who hears My word and believes in Him who sent
Me has everlasting life, and shall not come into judgment,
but has passed from death into life.

JOHN 5:24 NKJV

*O*My little ones, you are the apple of My eye, I will guard you
from harm. Never let the fears that are common to the world
creep into your hearts, for you are not of the world, and you
need not fear the things that plague the minds of the ungodly.

You need not fear the coming judgment, for if your sins
have been confessed and forgiven and cleansed by the blood
of Jesus, you will not be condemned, because you are already
passed from death into eternal life. You need not fear the Day
of Judgment. It is sent to try the world, and you are not of the
world, My little children.

What do I fear?

Only by a Person

from *Progress of Another Pilgrim*

I am the living bread which came down from heaven:
if any man eat of this bread, he shall live for ever:
and the bread that I will give is my flesh,
which I will give for the life of the world.

JOHN 6:51

I will bless you, My people, when your hearts turn to Me in earnestness and sincerity. From where shall your help come, except from the Lord? You search in vain for satisfaction from your worldly possessions.

Your soul can be nourished only by a person—not by any thing—and the only person adequate to meet the hunger of your soul is the Person of the Lord Jesus Christ, through the ministry of the blessed Holy Spirit.

Where is my heart turned?

Safety in God's Will

from *Come Away My Beloved*

If anyone is a worshiper of God and
does His will, He hears him.

JOHN 9:31 NKJV

*M*y will is not a place, but a condition. Do not ask Me where and when, but ask Me how. You will discover blessing in every place, and any place, if your spirit is in tune with Me.

I direct every motion of your life, as the ocean bears a ship. Your will and intelligence may be at the helm, but divine providence and sovereignty are stronger forces. You can trust Me, knowing that any pressure I bring to bear upon your life is initiated by My love.

Move on steadily, and know that the waters that carry you are the waters of My love and My kindness, and I will keep you on the right course.

What course is my life on?

Stay Pliable in My Hand

from *Come Away My Beloved*

I have come that they may have life,
and that they may have it more abundantly.

JOHN 10:10 NKJV

My child, be quick to obey. For the moving of My Spirit may at times be inconvenient to the flesh, and may at other times be diametrically opposed to reason, but obey Me regardless of the cost. You will always be amply repaid for any sacrifice with an abundance of blessing.

I will not force you to make the choice, nor make My will inescapable. There will always be an easier way open to you, one that will seem more reasonable, involving less risk. I have calculated the risk to test and develop your faith as well as your obedience, and in the choosing process, I give you an opportunity to prove your love for Me.

Be sensitive to My Spirit.

How sensitive am I to the Spirit?

Put Off the Self-Life

from *Progress of Another Pilgrim*

If ye know these things,
happy are ye if ye do them.

JOHN 13:17

---

*B*e aware of My presence. Your receptivity is dulled by undue involvement in unimportant pastimes. I need your full attention, yes, I need complete dedication.

These are the closing hours of this dispensation, and I am calling all My chosen to put off the self-life and to walk in the Spirit. This is not a new message. It was the message of the apostles; indeed, it was the message of Jesus. It was also the message of the Psalms and Proverbs, insofar as they emphasize uncompromising loyalty to the truth, and outward actions that are consistent with inward convictions.

How might my self-life be stunting my spiritual growth?

The Spirit of Life

from *Dialogues with God*

Greater works than these shall he do;
because I go unto my Father.

JOHN 14:12

———•◦•———•◦•———•◦•———

*R*esist not My Spirit, and set not a limit upon My movings.
Yield Me complete control, and hold not back, and thou
shalt break forth and yield an hundredfold.

My Spirit is the Spirit of Life, and I am in thee and upon thee
that thou shouldst not be barren nor unfruitful; and whomso-
ever thou touchest in faith shall feel My quickening power. Life
shall rise out of death, yea, Eternal Life out of spiritual death.

Is this not even greater than My servant Lazarus?

For I said, "Greater works than these shall he do; because I
go unto my Father" (John 14:12).

The world seeth Me not—but ye see Me, and because I live, ye
shall live also.

How do I resist the Spirit?

Rewards of Devotion

from *On the Highroad of Surrender*

He who has My commandments and keeps them, it is he who
loves Me. And he who loves Me will be loved by My Father,
and I will love him and manifest Myself to him.

JOHN 14:21 NKJV

*A*s your soul turns to worship, let it be with one supreme
desire: to bring Me your love. Eternity will be a time of rejoicing because all will love Me and find expression for their love.
This is not a selfish demand on My part. I can ask of you a full
portion, yes, unlimited devotion, because I am a giver, not a
taker, and you will always find yourself enriched beyond your
expectations whenever you give yourself to me in even a very
limited way.

I ask you to give only to bless you more.

When have I experienced God's blessing through obedience?

Renew Your Vows

from *Come Away My Beloved*

He who has My commandments and keeps them, it is he who loves Me. And he who loves Me will be loved by My Father, and I will love him and manifest Myself to him.

JOHN 14:21 NKJV

*T*here is a day coming when you will say, "I have waited in vain for the Lord." You will wait for Me to speak, and you will hear only the whistling of the wind. But I tell you now, I am never silent; you are deaf. I am always speaking, but I do not find your ear attuned to listen.

You will sit alone in a desolate place and grieve in your loneliness; but it will not be that I have left you, but that you have become insensitive to My presence.

Confess your coldness, and draw near to Me. Renew your vows, and I will revive your ministry.

How have I been insensitive to God's presence?

Strivings Hinder

Jesus answered and said unto him, If a man love me,
he will keep my words: and my Father will love him, and we
will come unto him, and make our abode with him.

JOHN 14:23

*M*y people are drifting like a boat with empty sails. But I
shall blow, saith the Lord; yes, I shall cause a mighty wind to
rise, and the sails shall be filled, and the Spirit shall drive you
forward. You shall rejoice in Me and praise My Name.

In your own power you can accomplish nothing whatsoever
in the kingdom of God. I need your submission, but I do not
need your help.

All strivings only hinder. Love is the only telling contribution you can make toward the perfecting of your soul.

Am I striving or submitting?

The Glory of My Presence

from *Dialogues with God*

My peace I give unto you: not as the world giveth,
give I unto you. Let not your heart be troubled,
neither let it be afraid.

JOHN 14:27

I will speak words of comfort and words of cheer to My
people.

Mine eyes behold, and Mine ears are open, and lo, all
through the night have I stood watch.

Through the darkness have I set limits for thy protection,
and lo, the enemy cannot break through the lines. For I have
set a limit to his power, and I have curtailed his activities.

I am in the midst of My people to give them peace. I shall
dine with them at the table, though countless hosts encamp
round about.

I shall cover them with My almighty hand.

How much of God's peace am I enjoying?

The Shadow of My Hand

from *On the Highroad of Surrender*

Peace I leave with you, My peace I give to you;
not as the world gives do I give to you.
Let not your heart be troubled, neither let it be afraid.

JOHN 14:27 NKJV

---

*P*eace, My child, is the shadow of My hand. When your soul is at rest, it is because you are consciously aware of My presence. You do not need to seek peace. As you realize My nearness, you will discover that I am there, in the center of your worship, for to seek Me is to desire to worship Me. Finding Me, you have no need to seek peace, for I Myself am your peace.

Is my soul at rest?

The Father's Husbandry

from *Progress of Another Pilgrim*

I am the true vine, and my Father is the husbandman.

JOHN 15:1

*F*aith, meekness, temperance: these are fruits that mature slowly, and they are perfected by the careful husbandry of the Father. There is a kind of faith that is a gift of God. This is believing faith for initial salvation. The faith which is produced within you as fruit of the Holy Spirit is a faith operating in the life of the believer to the end that he becomes a productive vehicle for the doing of the Father's work. Yes, and this fruit of meekness goes beyond mildness of temperament, even to an acceptance of injustice. It is not only patient, but gracious— returning good for evil. This is verily a divine fruit. This you may experience as you yield fully to My Spirit within.

What kind of fruit am I bearing?

Fulfillment

from *Progress of Another Pilgrim*

Herein is my Father glorified, that ye bear much fruit;
so shall ye be my disciples.

JOHN 15:8

*E*very door that I open, you shall pass through. My Spirit shall speak, and you shall utter that which is given unto you.

You have been like a green plant. Now I would have you put forth blossoms. The flowering is a symbol of the manifestation of the Spirit. Yes, it is even more; it is fulfillment of original purpose. It is destiny. It is the ultimate end to which it was designated by the Creator. Anything less would be failure and disappointment.

Only to have life is not enough. Fulfillment is that for which I am waiting, yes, the manifestation of My sons and daughters as they come to maturity and as they produce that for which I created them.

How am I fulfilling God's purpose in my life?

Pretense Will Not Worship

from *On the Highroad of Surrender*

When He, the Spirit of truth, has come,
He will guide you into all truth.

JOHN 16:13 NKJV

———————

*O*ut of much solitude comes a depth of understanding I cannot give to the one who pulls the world about himself as a blanket to cover his nakedness or closes himself in with noises to prevent hearing the emptiness of his own soul. Maturity comes in silence.

Only prayer furnishes the soul with nourishment, but prayer itself must be born of singleness of heart. Pretense will not enter the gate of worship. Pretense will stand outside and flaunt its own self-proclaimed piety. I would have you true and honest. Better to be a sinner and confess it than to profess purity you do not possess.

Search your heart in the light of My Word. Let the Holy Spirit give insight.

How true and honest is my heart?

The Healing Power of Joy

from *Come Away My Beloved*

You will be sorrowful, but your sorrow
will be turned into joy.
JOHN 16:20 NKJV

*D*istress of soul and grief of heart can only bring on
destruction of body. Joy alone is a healer, and you can have it
in the darkest hour if you will force your soul to rise to me in
worship and adoration.

Bring Me your sorrow, and watch for the sunrise of the
resurrection. Truly there comes a morning when hope is
reborn and life finds new beginning. Wait for it as tulip bulbs
anticipate the spring. The rarest blooms are enhanced by
the coldness of winter. The snow plays her part in producing
spring's pageant. But when the blossoms break through, we
do not then turn back to thoughts of winter, but instead, we
look ahead to the full joys of the coming summer.

What sorrows can I trade for God's joy?

Union of Spirit

from *Progress of Another Pilgrim*

I in them, and thou in me, that they may be made perfect in one; and that the world may know that thou hast sent me, and hast loved them, as thou hast loved me.

JOHN 17:23

There is a flow of divine life, and as you enter into it, you shall find victory. If you long to see your own personal wishes subjugated to the will and purposes of God, let your heart be at rest. For this union of your spirit with My Spirit and of your will and My will shall come as simply and easily as rain falling, if you can learn this one secret, that is, how to lose yourself in the flow of My life as I live within you.

Am I truly united with God's Spirit?

You Cannot Weary My Love

from *Come Away My Beloved*

Then saith he to Thomas, Reach hither thy finger, and behold my hands; and reach hither thy hand, and thrust it into my side: and be not faithless, but believing.

JOHN 20:27

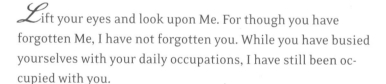

*L*ift your eyes and look upon Me. For though you have forgotten Me, I have not forgotten you. While you have busied yourselves with your daily occupations, I have still been occupied with you.

My little children, you cannot weary My love. You may grieve My heart, but My love is changeless, infinite. I long for you to turn to Me. My hands are full of blessings that I desire to give you. I long to hear your voice. You speak much with others—O speak to Me! I have so much to tell you.

How often do I speak with God?

Break Loose the Fetters

from *Come Away My Beloved*

But you shall receive power when the Holy Spirit has
come upon you; and you shall be witnesses to Me...
to the end of the earth.

ACTS 1:8 NKJV

*W*ith a strong and mighty hand I will bring My people out.
Yes, as I brought the children of Israel out from the bondage
of Egypt and Pharaoh, with a yet greater form of liberation I
will bring My people out from under the yoke of false prophets and the shackles of legalism. Do not be afraid to follow Me.
For one of these days the curtain will be drawn, the heavens
will be rolled back, the canopy of the sky as you know it will
be lifted away, and the Son of Man shall be revealed in power
and great glory.

Break loose the fetters. Cast off the fears. Walk forth in the
conquering strength of My Holy Spirit.

What fears bind me?

The Dynamic of Miracles

from *Progress of Another Pilgrim*

But ye shall receive power, after that the Holy Ghost
is come upon you: and ye shall be witnesses unto
me both in Jerusalem, and in all Judaea, and in Samaria,
and unto the uttermost part of the earth.

ACTS 1:8

⊘ My child, lie quietly in My hand. The dynamic of miracles
is here. Your own weakness is of no consequence, for I would
vest you with My power. Your insignificance shall be swallowed up in My Presence.

My Presence is all about you, even all through you. Unless
you resist Me, you cannot fail, for I cannot fail and you are in
Me, kept by the power of God. Strengthen your heart with this
truth.

How quiet am I in God's hand?

Give Yourself to Prayer and the Word

from *Progress of Another Pilgrim*

But we will give ourselves continually to prayer,
and to the ministry of the word.

Acts 6:4

⸺•┼•⸺ ⸺•┼•⸺ ⸺•┼•⸺

*G*ive yourself to a life of prayer and much careful study of the Word, that you may be able to give My message with clarity and the unction of the Holy Spirit.

Dispose of nonessentials. Concentrate your thoughts and intentions upon Jesus Christ, and in Him seek your wisdom and comfort. I will open avenues to aid you, for this is My will for you, and you can know that I will always make a way for the performance of My will in your life once you have set your goal to be obedient to My commands. Is it not written that I give you the desires of your heart? Give yourself to the desire, and I shall give Myself to the fulfillment.

What do I give myself to?

Expect the Unexpected

from *Come Away My Beloved*

Then Philip went down to the city of Samaria
and preached Christ to them. And the multitudes with
one accord heeded the things spoken by Philip, hearing
and seeing the miracles which he did.

ACTS 8:5-6 NKJV

My child, let Me speak to you, and let My Spirit direct your life. I may lead you in unexpected ways, and ask things of you that are startling, but I will never guide you amiss.

Do not walk according to your natural reasoning, but obey the promptings of the Spirit, and be obedient to My voice.

You shall go as Philip went—at the direction of the Spirit—into the places that are out of the way, and bring light on My Word to those who are in need.

Stay in an attitude of prayer and faith, and I will do all the rest.

What is my attitude?

Anticipate Surprises

from *Progress of Another Pilgrim*

And the angel of the Lord spake unto Philip, saying,
Arise, and go toward the south unto the way that goeth
down from Jerusalem unto Gaza, which is desert.

ACTS 8:26

*O*My child, be obedient. I have purposes for you. I have a
ministry for you. Look not to any man to open this door. I not
only open doors, but more often than otherwise, I create the
place of service. I make My own plans, and in order to reach
the souls for whom I am concerned, I lead in new paths and
down unpaved roads.

One Bible example of this is the account of Philip and his
witness to the eunuch crossing the desert.

Be prepared for the unexpected, and anticipate surprises if
you deign to follow Me.

How prepared am I to serve God in new ways?

The Ways of the Spirit

from *On the Highroad of Surrender*

And the men who journeyed with him stood speechless,
hearing a voice but seeing no one.

ACTS 9:7 NKJV

Do not grieve My Spirit and do not quench His power when
He is moving in your own or another vessel. My purifying
work is being done in the sacred moments when My anointing
is resting upon a soul. Be aware that as a witness, you stand
on holy ground, and reverence should be your attitude.

I reveal to each individual what is necessary for his own
soul's progress. Others do not need to know. Like Saul on the
road to Damascus, to him were spoken clear words, while others heard only a sound. Even so, I speak clearly to the one who
is slain in the Spirit. Others need not know nor question.

How is my soul's progress?

A Beautiful Work

from *Come Away My Beloved*

He is a chosen vessel of Mine to bear My name.

ACTS 9:15 NKJV

*Y*ou are Mine. You are not your own. With a great price I have purchased you for Myself. If you will listen to Me, I will reveal to you more fully so that you may know more clearly how vital you are to My purpose. There is work to be done, and I need you as a vessel through which to work. Not a vassal, but a vessel. I want to do a beautiful work.

There will be inconveniences to be borne, self-pleasing to be laid aside, sacrifices and pain—but what a blessed reward I have in store! Yes, in store for you, if you are able to let Me use you the way I desire.

Lo, I wait for you. Come to Me.

How willing am I to be God's vessel?

Attitude Determines Outcome

from *On the Highroad of Surrender*

I was not disobedient to the heavenly vision.

ACTS 26:19 NKJV

*I*n every situation, you have a confrontation of duty. You can, by total dedication of your own being, turn every experience into a spiritual victory. It is the attitude with which you approach any day that will determine its outcome.

You are not a helpless pawn on a board. You are a child of God with prerogatives for accomplishing His will, not your own. Let this help to bring you guidance when you are in doubt.

Be about your Father's business. There will always be plenty of other people occupied with the affairs of the world.

What spiritual victories am I experiencing?

Hidden Resources

from *Progress of Another Pilgrim*

And not only so, but we glory in tribulations also:
knowing that tribulation worketh patience.

ROMANS 5:3

———————

There is no alternative for faith. You have need of testings
to develop your character. There is no other way. Avoidance
of stress engenders weakness. Accept the trials of life as they
come, and look for the good in each. Only in this way can you
advance and grow in stature.

Only through much self-discipline and self-denial can you
gain the victory.

It is only through the power of My Spirit within you that
you shall be able to tap hidden resources that have power to
sustain you above yourself. Therefore you are not dependent
upon nor limited by the level of your own strength of character, but you may rise above it and lift your own actions up into
My divine pattern for you.

What trials are currently helping me to grow?

Kindness

from *On the Highroad of Surrender*

Now hope does not disappoint, because the love
of God has been poured out in our hearts
by the Holy Spirit who was given to us.

ROMANS 5:5 NKJV

*I*n tenderness, My child, lies the greatest strength that can come to the human heart. Kindness is like a rose, which though easily crushed and fragile, yet speaks a language of silent power. It is the same power that lies in the eyes of one who loves. It is the power that moves the hands of those who give alms.

Beauty comes to the inner soul as tenderness becomes the outer expression. Those who find it have captured the atmosphere of heaven and have brought to their human relationships the essence of God's holy love.

*How much tenderness do I offer to those
seeking God's kingdom?*

Endurance

from *On the Highroad of Surrender*

Now hope does not disappoint, because the love
of God has been poured out in our hearts
by the Holy Spirit who was given to us.

ROMANS 5:5 NKJV

---

*M*y child, do not flinch under My disciplines. I never send
more than you can endure. Can you accept the cup of suffering as readily as you embrace joy? You can do so in greater
degrees as your trust in Me increases.

My love never fails, even when it brings you pain. It is in
the patient endurance of affliction that the soul is seasoned
with grace. It is a barren life that holds only happiness. Saints
are not nurtured by levity. Hope does not spring from good
fortune.

How have I responded to God's disciplines?

Desire Holiness

from *Make Haste My Beloved*

For sin shall not have dominion over you:
for ye are not under the law, but under grace.

ROMANS 6:14

—◆——◆——◆—

*Y*ou should never abandon your desire for holiness because of your failures. You judge yourself incurably sinful. I see you as potentially pure. When you can look upon your own soul with compassion, you will know that My spirit has worked a work of grace in your heart, and you shall be lifted above despair. You shall have a song of praise on your lips and a shout of victory in your heart.

Do I desire holiness or give in to despair?

Strengthening Power

from *Dialogues with God*

For that which I do I allow not: for what I would,
that do I not; but what I hate, that do I.

ROMANS 7:15

━━◆┼◆━━━━━◆┼◆━━━━━◆┼◆━━

*Y*ou have heard of Me by the hearing of the ear, but long to see Me. Yea, you desire to behold Me daily in the light of fresh revelation, yea, by the illumination of the Spirit who dwelleth within. You need the daily inward strengthening of the new man in the power of My might, to be enabled to walk in obedience to My commands.

You know to do good but continually battle the tendencies of your human nature to do otherwise. For the flesh resisteth the progress of the Spirit (Romans 7:15-25). But as Paul, you make your confession: Thanks be unto God Who giveth us the victory through our Lord Jesus Christ!

Am I daily strengthened by Him?

My Energizing Spirit

from *Dialogues with God*

But if the Spirit of him that raised up Jesus from the dead
dwell in you, he that raised up Christ from the dead shall also
quicken your mortal bodies by his Spirit that dwelleth in you.

ROMANS 8:11

*O*My child, I will help thee. I am more real than all thy
desires or thy fears. Yea, My Spirit is a quickening, life-giving
Spirit. I come to be thy Light.

In My presence there is no darkness. Have ye not read that
in the Eternal City there is no need of candle, nor of the sun
or moon, because the Lamb is the Light of it? Surely if I can
brighten all of Eternity, I have ample supply to flood thy heart
and mind and thy body with My mighty power, My light, and
My love—My deep joy and My energizing Spirit.

Ye need not depend upon thine own limited strength and
endurance.

What do I depend on?

Only Yield the Vessel

from *Progress of Another Pilgrim*

For as many as are led by the Spirit of God,
they are the sons of God.

ROMANS 8:14

---

*B*e obedient to the still, small voice. It will engage your soul in devotion. It will give you direction. It will revive and enlighten your own spirit and imbue your soul with divine love.

I am in your midst, dwelling deep within your being. You need not search for Me any further away than your own heart. I have come to reside there by your own invitation. Do not turn outward again and ignore Me, but look in and know that what I give you to share with others will very truly be not ministering of yourself, but the flowing forth of My Spirit shall move through you and speak through you. Only yield your vessel. He is your victory.

When have I heard God's still, small voice?

Pray and Walk in the Spirit

from *Progress of Another Pilgrim*

For as many as are led by the Spirit of God,
they are the sons of God.

ROMANS 8:14

*L*o, I have admonished you to pray in the Spirit, but do not forget that I have also commanded you to WALK in the Spirit, and this I expect not part of the time, but all the time.

The need is critical, the hour is late, and I am calling for full commitment from My own. You have desired to be chosen. Having been chosen, I would have you understand that I expect far more of you than of those who are not.

How am I praying and walking in His Spirit?

Turbulence, a Warning Signal

from On the Highroad of Surrender

For as many as are led by the Spirit of God,
they are sons of God.

ROMANS 8:14

One step at a time, My child. When I lead, there is no confusion. Never let others lead. Your need for confirmation will be answered by the Spirit. My Holy Spirit meets your every need. If it is wisdom that you seek, you will receive it if you draw upon Him. He resides within you to be your all. Never bypass this infinite supply of all goodness. Never move into a new situation until you are at peace about it within your own soul. My Spirit harmonizes all action. If you sense discord or turbulence, know that there is a spiritual battle already on the scene. Let it be a warning signal. Look for the root of it, and do not blindly forge ahead.

Is God's Spirit or another leading me?

The Forces of Intercession

from *Progress of Another Pilgrim*

Likewise the Spirit also helpeth our infirmities:
for we know not what we should pray for as we ought:
but the Spirit itself maketh intercession for us
with groanings which cannot be uttered.

ROMANS 8:26

*B*ring the struggles within your soul to Me in prayer. It is the movement within you of the forces of intercession which you are feeling. It is not a personal struggle. The resolutions shall come as you pray, not as you search for wisdom as an end in itself.

Prayer has brought more illumination than books. Seek Me, and you shall know. You shall understand more than you dream possible, and your inner peace shall deepen.

What struggles should I bring to God?

The Vineyard of Prayer

from *Come Away My Beloved*

Now He who searches the hearts knows what the mind of the Spirit is, because He makes intercession for the saints according to the will of God.

ROMANS 8:27 NKJV

My child, the days are heavy with burdens that need to be borne upon the shoulders of faithful prayer warriors. Where are those who are willing to make themselves available for this ministry? You cannot in yourself lay this ministry upon your soul, but you can make room in your life for time apart with Me; and as you place yourself at the disposal of the Holy Spirit, He will use you as a channel when the needs arise.

I am calling My Spirit-filled believers to labor in the vineyard of prayer. Rejoice to be granted the privilege of so sacred a task. Cherish it and cultivate it.

How can I cultivate my vineyard of prayer?

Victory in Adversity

from *On the Highroad of Surrender*

And we know that all things work together for good
to those who love God, to those who are the called
according to His purpose.

ROMANS 8:28 NKJV

*W*henever you experience pain, know that I am knocking at
the door of your heart.

Nothing should be of any real concern to you except your
relationship to Me and a right attitude toward others. Life
brings unpleasant circumstances, but I say unto you, I am in
the midst, causing all experiences, both pleasant and otherwise, to harmonize for your blessing and growth.

I do not shield you from hardship. I give you victory while
in the throes of adversity.

How is God working out His victory in my life?

Flee Compromise

from *On the Highroad of Surrender*

Nay, in all these things we are more than conquerors
through him that loved us.

ROMANS 8:37

O My people, the hour is late and the time for sleeping is past. Gird on the armor of truth and righteousness, and know that the battle is in full array.

Not by might nor by power, but by My Spirit shall you be victorious, so do not seek to outwit the enemy by fleshly strategy. Only as you go in the strength of the Lord shall you stand.

Flee compromise, for it leads always to defeat. The shed blood of Christ is your only protection. When you go into battle, go in My Name, and know that you go against an already-defeated foe.

Claim the victory, and know that it is yours as you act in faith, not doubting, not retreating, and not arbitrating with the enemy.

In what areas am I tempted to compromise?

Learn to Reign

from *Come Away My Beloved*

Nay, in all these things we are more than
conquerors through him that loved us.

ROMANS 8:37

---

*Y*ou are not qualified to be used for My purposes as long as you are being harassed by the enemy and I keep needing to rescue you from a constant parade of distressing predicaments. You are more than conquerors.

Rise up, then, and lay claim to the power that is yours, because I am in you, and you are in Me, and as I was in the world, so are you. I was victorious, and you too may be victorious. I withstood every encounter with the devil, and you, too, can stand against him. I healed the sick and wrested tortured bodies out of the grip of evil forces, and you, too, can do the same.

Learn to reign, for I have made you to become kings and priests.

How can I learn to reign?

The Righteous Remnant

from On the Highroad of Surrender

And it shall come to pass in the place where
it was said to them, "You are not My people,"
There they shall be called sons of the living God.

ROMANS 9:26 NKJV

---

*H*ear Me, O My people, and listen to My words. You give attention continually to the words of others. You listen, read, you study and ponder and consider multitudes of words that express only the thoughts of others who, like yourself, are searching for Truth. To search is not evil, but if you desire understanding, come directly to Me. Ask of Me. As the scriptures teach, if any seeks wisdom, let him ask of God, for He gives liberally (James 1:5).

Wait upon Me, and I will clarify things that are dark and puzzling to you.

Whose words do I listen to?

Remove the Barriers

from *On the Highroad of Surrender*

But to Israel he says: "All day long I have stretched
out My hands to a disobedient and contrary people."

ROMANS 10:21 NKJV

My children, over many barriers I call to you. Man has
erected walls that separate brothers, but you, My people, have
allowed many walls to separate yourselves from the full reve
lation of My glory.

I do not withhold Myself by choice, but you prevent Me
from fellowshipping with you. Curtains of doubt, fear, timidity, unrepentance, and many others hide My face from you so
that you cannot know Me.

I plead with you, yes, I cry out to you that before it is too
late you will turn to Me with no devices of self-defense, and
then can I open My heart to you and pour out My blessings.

What walls have separated me from God?

Counsel with Me

from *Progress of Another Pilgrim*

(According as it is written, God hath given them the
spirit of slumber, eyes that they should not see,
and ears that they should not hear;) unto this day.

ROMANS 11:8

$\mathcal{B}$e not disturbed by evildoers. They are in My hand to do as
I please, even as are the righteous. Do not be alarmed. All is
under My control. Stand upon My Word, and let your only support be your faith in Me. I Myself will hold you up and keep
you from swaying.

What goes on in the lives of others need not distress you. I
will deal with them. Walk in Me. Counsel with Me, and look to
Me alone for your direction and your encouragement.

Go your way in peace and in rejoicing. The Lord your God is
with you and will be your helper.

Do I look to God alone for direction?

True Holiness

from *On the Highroad of Surrender*

I beseech you therefore, brethren, by the mercies
of God, that you present your bodies a living sacrifice, holy,
acceptable unto God, which is your reasonable service.

ROMANS 12:1

*T*rue holiness, when wrought in you by My grace, is not an
end in itself. It is a transforming work by the Holy Spirit to
the end that My will may be accomplished through you. If
you are a flowing, vital part of My eternal purpose, you are
blessed. If you, by your willful disobedience, become a hindering factor, you suffer in accordance to the degree of your
rebellion.

Stretch forth the hand of faith. Set foot upon the territory
you wish to claim. I will move ahead of you and clear a path,
but you must be determined to follow closely, and to hold your
ground without wavering.

What territory do I wish to claim?

Your Body, a Living Sacrifice

from *Come Away My Beloved*

Present your bodies a living sacrifice, holy, acceptable unto
God, which is your reasonable service. And be not conformed
to this world: but be ye transformed by the renewing of
your mind, that ye may prove what is that good,
and acceptable, and perfect, will of God.

ROMANS 12:1–2

————————

*Y*ield Me your body as a living sacrifice, and do not be
conformed to the things of the world, but be transformed by
the renewal of your mind. Set your affections on things of the
Spirit, and do not be in bondage to the desires of the flesh. For
I have purchased you at great price. Yes, you are My special
possession and My treasure.

How can I become a "living sacrifice" to God?

Return unto Me

Do not be conformed to this world, but be transformed
by the renewing of your mind, that you may prove what
is that good and acceptable and perfect will of God.

ROMANS 12:2 NKJV

*R*eturn to Me, for I have sought after you, but you have continued on in pursuit of your own ways. I have called to you, but you have disregarded Me. I have placed obstacles in your path, but you have obstinately and determinedly forged on ahead.

Have you learned no wisdom? Have past lessons fled your mind?

Put down your anxieties, and trust Me for everything. You need nothing but what I am fully able to supply, with no effort on your part.

Come close to Me, and I will minister to you and revive your spirit.

Am I conformed to God's will or following my own?

Anxiety

from *On the Highroad of Surrender*

Rejoicing in hope, patient in tribulation,
continuing steadfastly in prayer.

ROMANS 12:12 NKJV

———•◦•————•◦•————•◦•———

*M*y child, when you are tired, do not be disheartened.
Most of your discouragement comes when you carry your own
burden, forgetting to call upon Me for help. Give Me everything, and quickly, for as soon as any heaviness of spirit sets
in, trust is crowded out. An atmosphere of anxiety or unhappiness is withering to faith.

Continual prayer will fortify your soul.

Is anything withering my faith today?

Righteousness, Peace, and Joy

from *On the Highroad of Surrender*

For the kingdom of God is not food and drink,
but righteousness and peace and joy in the
Holy Spirit. For he who serves Christ in these
things is acceptable to God and approved by men.

ROMANS 14:17-18 NKJV

---

*M*y people shall not languish in weakness, for I will be their strength.

No evil force can hold back My Spirit.

Believe Me and trust Me. You need not plot and scheme and plan. To doubt and to strive is to detain the Spirit. He needs not your help—only your submission. Give it willingly and gladly; yes, give it quickly, for the kingdom of God is righteousness, peace, and joy in the Holy Ghost, and you hinder the Spirit when these are not ruling your heart.

Am I striving or submitting?

Faith, a Perpendicular Operation

from *Progress of Another Pilgrim*

And he that doubteth is damned if he eat,
because he eateth not of faith:
for whatsoever is not of faith is sin.

ROMANS 14:23

—•÷•——— —•÷•——— —•÷•—

*B*e alert. Keep your thoughts always on Me. Give Me your trouble, whatever it may be. There is no disturbance big enough to warrant your distress, because anything committed to Me will be taken care of.

Be steadfast, and be one about whom it can be said that you truly live and walk by faith. I will be with you and help you, and I will be your strength.

No barrier shall stand in your way, because faith is a per-pendicular operation. Your faith reaches straight up to Me, and My power comes straight down upon the place of action.

What troubles can I give to God today?

You Are Violating My Will

from *Progress of Another Pilgrim*

We then that are strong ought to bear the
infirmities of the weak, and not to please
ourselves. Let every one of us please his
neighbour for his good to edification.

ROMANS 15:1-2

*M*y child, you are not where I would have you be. How can
I be pleased with you? "Love," it is written, "seeketh not her
own." But you have been pursuing your own ends, and this, to
Me, is folly. What you desire may be beautiful and good and
may constitute nothing that is harmful in itself; all the same,
you are violating My will and marring My pattern.

Are there any ways in which I'm violating
God's will in my life?

First Place

from *Come Away My Beloved*

Even Christ pleased not himself.

ROMANS 15:3

*E*very soldier must give first place to his obligation to the armed forces, and second place to his own private life and wishes. Even so you must do, if you would be My followers. Even so did Jesus during His earthly ministry. His entire life was subordinated to the Father's will.

How dare you risk allowing the flesh to manifest its desires? They can be only evil continually. No good thing can come out of a deceitful heart.

Only that generated within you by the Spirit of God can bring forth righteousness; do not be conformed to this world, but be transformed by the renewing of your mind, that you may personally discover what is the good and acceptable and perfect will of God.

Am I discovering God's perfect will?

An Open Vessel

from *On the Highroad of Surrender*

Now may the God of hope fill you with all joy
and peace in believing, that you may abound
in hope by the power of the Holy Spirit.

ROMANS 15:13 NKJV

—◦—◦◦—◦—— ◦◦◦ ——◦—◦◦—◦—

*B*e about My business. Hold back nothing from Me. The fullness of My blessing moves through the sensitivity of your soul. The callous block Me out. It is not that I do not care for them, but it is that I find no response.

Give Me an open vessel into which I may pour My Spirit. Though it be of clay, it shall overflow with glory.

How can I open myself to receive
God's Spirit?

Strength and Weakness

from *On the Highroad of Surrender*

But of Him you are in Christ Jesus, who became
for us wisdom from God—and righteousness and
sanctification and redemption—that, as it is written,
"He who glories, let him glory in the LORD."

1 CORINTHIANS 1:30-31 NKJV

*M*y Spirit within you, My child, is the source of your spiritual life and strength. Look not to your own natural abilities, for My Spirit empowers the one who would walk in faith, so that he who is weak need not despair, and he who feels himself to be strong shall learn not to boast; for I bring down the mighty and make strong the weak.

Do I look to myself or to God for my strength?

On the Waters of Sorrow

from *Come Away My Beloved*

> But as it is written: "Eye has not seen,
> nor ear heard, nor have entered into the heart
> of man the things which God has prepared
> for those who love Him."
>
> 1 CORINTHIANS 2:9 NKJV

My child, I am coming to you walking on the waters of the sorrows of your life; yes, above the sounds of the storm you shall hear My voice call your name.

You are never alone, for I am at your right hand. Never despair, for I am watching over and caring for you. Be not anxious. What seems to you to be at present a difficult situation is all part of My planning, and I am working out the details of circumstances so that I may bless you and reveal Myself to you in a new way.

What tempts me to feel despair or anxiety?

A Way of Triumph

from *Progress of Another Pilgrim*

But as it is written, Eye hath not seen, nor ear heard,
neither have entered into the heart of man, the things
which God hath prepared for them that love him.

1 CORINTHIANS 2:9

*N*ever be led by human reasoning. The day is coming when
you would have faltered but for the understanding I am giving
you now.

It is a way of triumph when it leads to fuller enlighten-
ment. When My presence is with you, you can know there is a
blessing in store. It shall open to you as you trust Me. It shall
be beautiful beyond your highest dreams.

Am I on the way of triumph?

Seek Me in the Hidden Places

from *Progress of Another Pilgrim*

But God hath revealed them unto us by his Spirit:
for the Spirit searcheth all things, yea, the deep things of God.
For what man knoweth the things of a man, save the spirit
of man which is in him? even so the things of God
knoweth no man, but the Spirit of God.

1 CORINTHIANS 2:10-11

*U*nderstanding comes not by outer observation but by inner revelation. I Myself will teach you. I Myself will open to you many mysteries. Fret not, neither set a limit as to what you may attain. I will communicate with you more and more, and at a deeper level of understanding, as you seek Me in the hidden places of your soul.

How deeply do I want to communicate with God?

Spiritual Awareness

from *Progress of Another Pilgrim*

Now we have received, not the spirit of the world,
but the spirit which is of God; that we might know
the things that are freely given to us of God.

1 CORINTHIANS 2:12

*A*s a child has eyesight, but only by teaching and study does he learn the art of reading, so likewise, what I do for you is to train you to comprehend intelligently that which you see in the Spirit.

The same principle applies in the other areas of spiritual awareness. Know that you have five avenues of spiritual operation, and let Me be your teacher and guide you into how to interpret the information that comes to you in these various ways.

Is God my only teacher and guide?

The Spiritual House

from *On the Highroad of Surrender*

For we are God's fellow workers;
you are God's field, you are God's building.

1 CORINTHIANS 3:9 NKJV

---

*O*ver many obstacles I move in the lives of My children, bringing to pass the full fruition of My plans for each one. Each life is like the building of a house. Much labor is required in preparing the foundation. The most beautiful home will not endure if the foundation is crooked or weak. I build slowly and carefully, and you need patience, for years may pass before the superstructure of your spiritual house begins to take shape.

The swiftness with which I build is determined by your reception of truth. Truth assimilated generates creativity. Obedience practiced generates productivity. Therefore, a teachable spirit and determined desire to do My will hastens the working of My purposes in you.

How receptive am I to God's truth?

Share Courage

from *On the Highroad of Surrender*

To the weak I became as weak, that I might win
the weak. I have become all things to all men,
that I might by all means save some.

1 CORINTHIANS 9:22 NKJV

*Y*our compassion for other souls will be in direct proportion
to your own sense of need. Self-dependence makes it difficult
to comprehend the timidity of the weak. Though you may
have gained a measure of strength, remember that it was not
native; it has been cultivated through a multitude of experiences, and you can remember many times when you were
fearful and trembling. Other souls are still in the place of fear
and desperation. Be always ready and willing to stand with
them in that place and share your faith and courage, yes, even
as many others shared with you in your times of need!

When have I stood with the weak?

Integrity—a Sacred Charge

from *Progress of Another Pilgrim*

Whether therefore ye eat, or drink,
or whatsoever ye do, do all to the glory of God.

1 CORINTHIANS 10:31

There is a way that you must go because of faithfulness
to Me. All you do, let it be as unto Me. Never do anything as
pleasing men, but do all for Me and for My glory. Thus, and
only thus, can your heart be kept at peace, and only in this
way can you honor Me and bring forth fruit.

My Name is as perfume. Let it ever be upon your lips. Speak
of Me often, and all other relationships shall be hallowed.

The integrity of your own heart is your most sacred charge.
Guard this with utmost care.

How often do I speak of Jesus?

True Dedication

from *Progress of Another Pilgrim*

But when we are judged, we are chastened of the Lord,
that we should not be condemned with the world.

1 CORINTHIANS 11:32

I am calling you aside into a walk of Faith. There is no self-denial possible without full surrender. There are forms of self-punishment that cloak themselves in the robes of dedication but are really false expressions and not true piety. Only I can lay upon you a true spirit of humility and dedication. Only My love can motivate a genuine self-sacrifice.

Do not deceive yourself. Let Me try your motives and probe the depths of your heart. My intention is to bless you, not to cause you unnecessary suffering.

Go your way in peace, knowing I have promised to perfect that which concerneth you, and My ways are ways of wisdom.

When has God revealed the true motives of my heart?

The Spiritual Senses

from *Progress of Another Pilgrim*

But the manifestation of the Spirit
is given to every man to profit withal.

1 CORINTHIANS 12:7

Did I not promise that I would send a rain of refreshing?
I will surely fill your vessel with a mighty downpour of My
reviving Spirit. I will quicken your senses and you shall hear
in the Spirit, and you shall speak in the Spirit, and you shall
discern in the Spirit. You shall verily feel in the same way. For
as man has five natural senses, regenerated souls have five
spiritual senses, and every alert, healthy believer should have
these operating.

The power is given you already. Exercise it and let Me
educate you along these lines.

How do I exercise the Spirit's power?

Spiritual Riches

from *On the Highroad of Surrender*

But earnestly desire the best gifts.

1 CORINTHIANS 12:31 NKJV

*R*ejoice in Me, for truly I am all you need. You can never ask beyond My power to provide.

Ask then, with complete confidence, but in all you desire, let it be for the enrichment of your soul. Seek not the treasures of the world, for they are transient.

Learn the value of spiritual riches, and set your heart to their attainment. You may lay your natural talents aside and know that as I bestow upon you spiritual enablements, I will use in a new way and in accordance with My highest purposes whatever lies within you of native abilities, or I may give you something entirely new. Nothing is wasted in the Spirit.

How can I seek my soul's enrichment?

The Motivation of Love

from *Progress of Another Pilgrim*

Though I speak with the tongues of men and
of angels, and have not charity, I am become
as sounding brass, or a tinkling cymbal.

1 CORINTHIANS 13:1

*M*any a life could be simplified and enriched by doing less
and loving more. Indeed, all that is ever done, if not motivated
by divine love, is in vain. It is worse than doing nothing, for it
is potentially destructive.

There are those who have risen to fame through their noble
acts, only to fall into shame and disrepute because of a bitter
spirit.

Is all I do motivated by love?

Purity of Motive

from *Progress of Another Pilgrim*

Though I speak with the tongues of men and of angels,
and have not charity, I am become as sounding brass,
or a tinkling cymbal.

1 CORINTHIANS 13:1

*R*egardless of how sacred may be the nature of a ministry,
it may be marred by a heart that is selfish or impure. Whatever does not spring out of pure love for God and love for your
fellowman becomes only a hollow noise.

The work of the Kingdom suffers delay for lack of laborers;
but let those who desire to serve continually offer up a yielded
vessel that I may cleanse it from sin and perfect it in righteousness and fill it with love. Only thus is it possible for any
man to enter into the activity of the Spirit of God in a way that
furthers the divine purpose.

When has my heart been selfish or impure?

On Privacy

from *On the Highroad of Surrender*

Love suffers long and is kind; love does not envy;
love does not parade itself, is not puffed up;
does not behave rudely, does not seek its own,
is not provoked, thinks no evil.

1 CORINTHIANS 13:4-5 NKJV

*D*o not allow your thoughts to pursue in curiosity what you do not understand in the lives of others.

To violate the spiritual privacy of another is a greater breach of ethics than to invade his house uninvited. Rest assured that if your friendship warrants, he will share with you as he deems wise, and what he appears to withhold, you will (if your affection for him is genuine) have the confidence that he is withholding as much for your own good as for his.

Love believes only the best. There is no more eloquent way to express love and respect for another than by allowing him full liberty of independent action.

In what relationships do I need to protect privacy?

Flesh and Blood

from *Come Away My Beloved*

Now this I say, brethren, that flesh and blood
cannot inherit the kingdom of God; neither
doth corruption inherit incorruption.

1 CORINTHIANS 15:50

I ask you not to do, but to be.

For whatsoever is of the flesh is flesh, but when you allow My Spirit to have free course, then those things that shall be accomplished both within and through you will be truly the life of God.

For My Spirit is the Spirit of Life, and My Spirit is the motivating power of Divine energy.

All else is death. As it is written, "Flesh and blood cannot inherit the Kingdom of God" (see 1 Corinthians 15:50).

Neither can man through any endeavor of his own, however holy his purpose, produce this life, which does not exist apart from the direct activity of the Spirit of God.

How freely do I allow the Spirit to move in my life?

I Will Bring the Victory

from *Come Away My Beloved*

Thanks be to God, who gives us the victory
through our Lord Jesus Christ.

1 CORINTHIANS 15:57 NKJV

My child, have I ever failed you? Have I not been your refuge and your strong defense? Fear not. My purposes will be fulfilled in spite of your weaknesses, if in your need you rely on My strength.

My will shall be done regardless of the flaws in your life, if you count on the power of My righteousness. I glory in over-ruling the prevailing circumstances, and I take pleasure in bringing victories in those places where no victory is any-where in sight.

Count on My coming.

Ask for the victory. I will come and bring it.

How often do I ask God for the victory?

The Course Lies Dead Ahead

from *Progress of Another Pilgrim*

But thanks be to God, which giveth us the
victory through our Lord Jesus Christ.

1 CORINTHIANS 15:57

The time will come that you will say, "Surely the Lord was in this place and I knew it not." My Spirit broods upon the waters, even upon the waters of difficulty, and I shall bring out of the chaotic condition in your life a trophy and a witness of My grace. Be not dismayed, neither be turned aside. Set your heart with even greater diligence to follow the Spirit. Others may find Me and lose Me again. Be not discouraged. What navigator would set his course by the location of other ships? You have a harbor to make, and you have a course to follow that lies dead ahead.

Is my course set on God or other ships?

The Door Is Open

from *On the Highroad of Surrender*

For a great and effective door has opened to me,
and there are many adversaries.

1 CORINTHIANS 16:9 NKJV

*M*y child, the door is open. You shall go through by My grace and in My strength. Never gauge the possibilities of victory by examining your own strength. I am your Life, your Purity, your Wisdom, and your Strength. You have built faith for many years through a knowledge of and confidence in My Word. Now, I say unto you, Put it into operation by walking in the path of action. Only in this way can you come into the full possession of your inheritance.

Move out, and trust Me as you go.

Give Me your yieldedness, your love, and a pure desire. I will do the rest.

What door has God opened for me?
Am I ready to walk through it?

A Way-Preparer

from *Progress of Another Pilgrim*

Watch ye, stand fast in the faith,
quit you like men, be strong.

1 CORINTHIANS 16:13

---

*B*e tolerant of all, at whatever stage of spiritual development they may be, but do not set your standards by theirs. I am moving, and I want you to be a way-preparer. Get into the front ranks, and hold your position. Never flinch. Certainly I can expect you never to turn coward and flee!

Give Me the privilege of sustaining you in the dangerous position. Think you not that I am well able to keep you there and adequately supply every needed grace?

How willing am I to step into God's front ranks?

Recognition and Focus

from *On the Highroad of Surrender*

But we all, with unveiled face, beholding as in a mirror
the glory of the Lord, are being transformed into the same
image from glory to glory, just as by the Spirit of the Lord.

2 CORINTHIANS 3:18 NKJV

*R*ecognition, My child, brings Me into focus. Your motives
concern Me, for I know that from pure motives spring good
works, just as a loving heart spontaneously prompts gentle
manners.

Recognition is the sight I give your inner eye to discern
distortion of My image in your own character. I do not say in
your brother's, but in your own! I would have your personality
patterns display My character, and wherever this fails to be so,
there is distortion of the image, and as others look to you for
guidance and inspiration, they do not see a clear image of Me.

How do others see God when they look at me?

Boundless Joy

from *Progress of Another Pilgrim*

But we have this treasure in earthen vessels, that the
excellency of the power may be of God, and not of us.

2 CORINTHIANS 4:7

*K*now in your heart that your vessel has been formed for
the purpose of shedding abroad the glory of God, and the Spirit ministers in you to the end that this may be accomplished.

Lo, I stand at your side to help, and you shall never need to
rely on your own strength or wisdom. As long as you bless and
honor Me, the rivers of life shall flow forth and your joy shall
be boundless.

How am I blessing and honoring God?

Saturate Your Soul in the Oil of the Spirit

from *Come Away My Beloved*

We are hard-pressed on every side, yet not crushed; we are perplexed, but not in despair; persecuted, but not forsaken.

2 CORINTHIANS 4:8–9 NKJV

The everlasting power of the Godhead is incarnate in My chosen ones. Is it not written that the kingdom of God dwells within you? I will bring to pass miracles—when you walk in uprightness and with mercy.

Come to Me with a clean heart and a right spirit, in sincerity, in honesty. Sin brings forth death, and any negative current flowing within your body will produce a steady regression.

Saturate your soul in the oil of the Holy Spirit, and keep your channel of communication always open to your Heavenly Father.

How clean is my heart—and how right is my spirit?

Thorns in the Nest

from *Progress of Another Pilgrim*

For our light affliction, which is but for a moment, worketh
for us a far more exceeding and eternal weight of glory.

2 CORINTHIANS 4:17

*I*n every situation, I control the forces that bear upon your
life. Do not question circumstances. Look to Me for an understanding of your inner responses.

Man looks upon the natural, physical world: My concern is
for your spiritual life, that virtues may develop in you. While
you are praying for a problem to be solved, a need to be met,
a thorn to be removed from your nest, I am watching for true
faith to express in the time of want, and I am waiting to see
when the thorns in the nest will cause you to move out and try
your unused wings.

When have I tried my spiritual "wings"?

Grief

from *On the Highroad of Surrender*

For our light affliction, which is but for a moment, is working
for us a far more exceeding and eternal weight of glory.

2 CORINTHIANS 4:17 NKJV

*B*ehold, there is a river of divine grace flowing beneath all
your need. Under your deepest sorrow moves My compassion
and My love. In a very real sense, you fathom the depth of My
own heart only to the extent that your heart is broken and
your inmost consciousness torn asunder by the pain of grief.

All things to grow require a proper climate. Love, if it is to
be given, must also be received. You are never so ready to accept My love as when you are experiencing anguish.

Never look upon trials and tests and disciplines as being
damaging. Whatever hurt they seem to bring is outweighed by
the blessing that follows.

When have I sought God's grace in grief?

Blessing in Adversity

from *Come Away My Beloved*

For our light affliction, which is but for a moment, worketh
for us a far more exceeding and eternal weight of glory.

2 CORINTHIANS 4:17

*A*dversities are a necessity. They are part of the pattern of life's pilgrimage for every individual, and who can escape them? But I say to you, that for those who walk in Me, and for those who are encircled by the intercessory prayers of My children, I will make of the suffering, yes, I will make of the trials a steppingstone to future blessing (see 2 Corinthians 4:17).

My arms are around you, and never have I loved you more! I will make you like a garden of fountains whose streams are fed by the mountain springs.

Am I looking at my trials or forward to God's blessing?

The Law of Plenty

from *On the Highroad of Surrender*

As poor, yet making many rich; as having nothing,
and yet possessing all things.

2 CORINTHIANS 6:10

*Y*es, My child, it matters not how little you have of the trea-sures of the world, for if you are blessed with the bounty of My grace, you shall be always a giver. There is no want for him who is My follower. There is no lack for him who has found that he can buy wine and milk without money and without price (Isaiah 55:1). He has found the law of plenty who has found Me as his source. He shall find abundance crowding his pathway as the blossoms of wild flowers crowd a hillside in springtime.

What kind of abundance crowds my path?

Recognize the Enemy

from *On the Highroad of Surrender*

Do not be unequally yoked together with
unbelievers. For what fellowship has righteousness with
lawlessness? And what communion has light with darkness?

2 CORINTHIANS 6:14 NKJV

My child, hear My voice, and let not the crafty words of a
stranger influence your thinking. My Word is all you need.
Study more and be filled with its wisdom that you may be for-
tified against insidious attacks of fallacious human reasoning. The high-sounding phrases of the humanist seem con-
vincing at times. But I say to you that any search that leads
you to your own self rather than to Me is of the devil. Either
take the offensive and win a victory for Me, or else sever the
connection. It would be better to retreat than to fall into a
snare. You have a full-scale assignment already at hand and
need all your resources for this.

What crafty words have distracted me from God's will?

No Compromise!

from *On the Highroad of Surrender*

Wherefore come out from among them, and be ye separate,
saith the Lord, and touch not the unclean thing;
and I will receive you.

2 CORINTHIANS 6:17

There are ways to witness without compromising, but there
is no way to compromise and at the same time effectively
witness. "Come out from among them, and be separate," says
the Word (2 Corinthians 6:17). This command has not been
altered. Come out! Those who seek the light will be drawn out
into the light. Those who remain in the darkness, it is written,
do so because they prefer the darkness to the light; and to go
back into darkness yourself, hoping to save them, will result
in giving the evil one the opportunity to assail your own soul.

You cannot have both—light and darkness—for "what accord
has Christ with Belial?" (2 Corinthians 6:14-18).

Am I separate or compromised?

Brokenness

from *On the Highroad of Surrender*

For godly sorrow produces repentance to salvation,
not to be regretted; but the sorrow of the
world produces death.

2 CORINTHIANS 7:10 NKJV

*B*rokenness comes only by the hand of the Holy Spirit upon the human heart. The storms of life may make shipwreck of a soul, but this may be purely destructive. The brokenness of spirit wrought by the hand of God becomes a constructive work. It is the godly sorrow unto repentance that brings Life.

The soul abounds in grace when prayer is its breath, and true prayer is born out of brokenness. This brokenness is contrition for sins, tenderness of feeling, and gratitude for grace. If you let it work in your heart, it will surely draw you closer and closer to Me.

When have I experienced true brokenness?

The Larger Life

from *Progress of Another Pilgrim*

And he said unto me, My grace is sufficient for thee:
for my strength is made perfect in weakness.
Most gladly therefore will I rather glory in my infirmities,
that the power of Christ may rest upon me.

2 CORINTHIANS 12:9

Never let your inadequacies be a handicap. Give them to
Me, and they will become My opportunity to demonstrate My
power operating through you. I would never have a chance
to help you if you were always self-sufficient and capable of
meeting every challenge.

Be ready to move in faith every time you sense inadequacy,
and in each experience, as you trust Me, you will experience
what is meant by "the larger life." I will fill all your lack with
My divine undertaking and bring you out with a testimony
unto My Name.

What personal inadequacies can I give to God today?

A Consuming Desire

from *On the Highroad of Surrender*

For do I now persuade men, or God?
Or do I seek to please men? For if I still pleased men,
I would not be a servant of Christ.

GALATIANS 1:10 NKJV

*I*f I lay not My hand upon you in punishment, come near.
Look into My eyes. Dare to draw close to My heart. You will
know surely My desire and purpose for you and shall grieve
more that you have displeased Me and caused Me grief than
that you may have forfeited some personal gain or blessing.
You will not view your spiritual walk as a challenge to be a
successful Christian in the eyes of others, but will have a consuming desire to please Me and bring only joy to My heart.

Whose approval do I seek in my Christian life?

Look Deeply

from *Progress of Another Pilgrim*

But I certify you, brethren, that the gospel which was
preached of me is not after man. For I neither received
it of man, neither was I taught it, but by the
revelation of Jesus Christ.

GALATIANS 1:11–12

*M*y child, look deeply within your heart, and much will
be revealed. Many things will become clear to you as you
look into your innermost being. It is a storehouse of wisdom.
Fear it not, for it is a deep pool of divine life because I Myself
reside there.

I will teach you in symbols as you learn to see in the Spirit.

Dismiss traditions. You disdain them but you still allow
yourself to be held in bondage to them. Drive out the bond-
man. Your spirit needs free course for expression. Do not
hamper it in ignorance.

Does tradition bind me, or am I free in God's Spirit?

I Anticipate Your Dependence on Me

from *Come Away My Beloved*

I have been crucified with Christ; it is no longer I who live,
but Christ lives in me; and the life which I now live in the
flesh I live by faith in the Son of God, who loved me
and gave Himself for me.

GALATIANS 2:20 NKJV

Do not wait to feel worthy, for no one is worthy of My blessings. My grace bypasses your shortcomings, and I give to My children because they ask of Me and because I love them. I give most liberally to those who ask the most of Me, for I love to have you depend on Me. As your Father, I anticipate your dependence on Me.

As you open your heart to Me, I will come to you. As you speak to Me, I will speak to you. As you reveal yourself to Me, I will reveal Myself to you.

How completely do I depend on God?

I Must Have Overcomers

from Come Away My Beloved

I have been crucified with Christ. . .the life which
I now live in the flesh I live by faith in the Son of God,
who loved me and gave Himself for me.

GALATIANS 2:20 NKJV

My children, the path where I will lead you is not a pleasant way, nor in accord with your selfish desires.

You have faith in Me; this is good, but faith without works is dead.

I must have overcomers through whom I may overcome. There is an enemy to be contested and defeated. My new life will become yours in direct proportion to your success in emptying your heart of self-will.

I know you cannot do this for yourself, but you must will it to be done. And as you will it, I will work with you and within you to bring it to pass.

What works have shown that my faith is real?

Ionospheric Christian Living

from *Progress of Another Pilgrim*

Stand fast therefore in the liberty wherewith
Christ hath made us free, and be not entangled
again with the yoke of bondage.

GALATIANS 5:1

Stay in the flexibility of the Spirit. Live in the faith realm, and let your thoughts soar freely in the open skies of faith, where the things not yet seen become real to you. Call it ionospheric Christian living, if you wish. It will free you from bondages to people. It will not give you an independent nor rebellious feeling toward others, but will liberate you so that you will no longer feel the need to struggle against these hindrances.

How free is my Christian life?

The Disciplines of Freedom

from *On the Highroad of Surrender*

Stand fast therefore in the liberty by which
Christ has made us free, and do not be entangled
again with a yoke of bondage.

GALATIANS 5:1 NKJV

O My people, I bring you out of bondage as rapidly as you are
able to cope with freedom. Hold fast in the liberty wherein I
have set you free and allow not anyone to bring you back into
subjection.

All sin is binding. In Christ is freedom, because in Him is
holiness. Your constant desire for purity is your safeguard
against the desire to return to the fleshpots and the slavery of
Egypt, which is always a symbol of the world. The world with
its desires passes away, but he who chooses to do the will of
God will live forever.

Am I standing fast in His freedom?

Magnificent Gift

from *Dialogues with God*

This I say then, Walk in the Spirit,
and ye shall not fulfil the lust of the flesh.

GALATIANS 5:16

---

*W*ell I know the instability of the human heart and natural affection. Thus I have supplied My own love to thy heart by the indwelling of My Holy Spirit. He it is who testifies of Me. He it is who prompts thy worship, who kindles the fires of devotion, who constantly draweth thee to Myself. For the carnal nature is hostile toward God, but the Holy Spirit within you ever crieth "Abba, Father," and He shall glorify Me at all times (Galatians 4:6, John 16:14).

Do ye long to love Me more deeply? Seek the infilling of My Holy Spirit. In this one magnificent gift, I have made full provision for thine every need.

What do I need the Spirit to help me with today?

Pride

from *On the Highroad of Surrender*

For the flesh lusts against the Spirit, and the Spirit
against the flesh; and these are contrary to one another,
so that you do not do the things that you wish.

GALATIANS 5:17 NKJV

Stand firm in your convictions against the contrary wind.
Every soul struggles against the elements. Thoughts of others
can come upon you like a storm at sea until your boat is well-
near swamped. Except for My grace, it would be destroyed.
But I am near at hand. Purify your heart so that I can be glorified in all your thoughts and actions.

I am concerned for your victory. You may have it as you fall
back into My arms and cease struggling.

Guard your heart from false values, and beware when man
begins to scheme and promote. I am not in it, says the Lord.

How firm are my convictions?

Grow Up in Me

from *Come Away My Beloved*

The fruit of the Spirit is love, joy, peace, longsuffering,
kindness, goodness, faithfulness, gentleness, self-control.

GALATIANS 5:22-23 NKJV

O My people, I have purposes for you that embrace eternity.
Before the creation of the worlds, I planned for your redemption.

Now that you are in Christ, you have My life abiding in you,
and you have become a new creation. Grow up in Me now, so that
you may develop into the full stature of men and women—even to
the measure of the fullness of Christ (see Ephesians 4:13).

My purpose was not simply to bring you into My family to remain as babies or children. I am concerned with your maturity,
with your growth in wisdom and knowledge of things pertain-
ing to Myself, with the perfection of your ministry, and with the
producing of the fruit of the Spirit in your life.

Where do I stand in spiritual maturity?

The Fruit of the Spirit

from *Progress of Another Pilgrim*

The fruit of the Spirit is love, joy, peace, longsuffering,
kindness, goodness, faithfulness, gentleness, self-control.

GALATIANS 5:22–23 NKJV

*M*y little children, I would speak to you concerning the
fruit of the Spirit. I would have you understand how My presence within you, My divine life, operating in your human
heart, creates the fruit of the Spirit.

It is not by self-effort that these heavenly attributes are
brought forth. Verily, the fruit of the Spirit is not native to the
world. The carnal man never brings forth this fruit.

Love, joy, and peace: these were natural to Jesus, but they
are foreign to man's fallen nature. You will never produce
them by seeking to suppress evil emotions. I am able to bring
them forth even from your inmost being as you allow Me to
live in you.

What spiritual fruit has grown in my life?

The Centrifugal Power of the Holy Spirit

from *Progress of Another Pilgrim*

But the fruit of the Spirit is love, joy, peace,
longsuffering, gentleness, goodness, faith, meekness,
temperance: against such there is no law.

GALATIANS 5:22-23

All kinds of contrivances will seek to throw you off balance. The centrifugal power of the Holy Spirit within you is ever seeking to draw you and keep you in the perfect divine pattern and form. Do not resist it. Rather, resist the pull of the external forces. In the language of the scriptures, it is the world, the flesh, and the devil which influence toward destruction and ugliness.

Only the divine Spirit of God—nothing else—can preserve your soul and life in the beauty of purity and the expression of grace.

Are purity and grace hallmarks of my life?

Set Your Heart to Follow to the End

from *Come Away My Beloved*

For he who sows to his flesh will of the flesh reap
corruption, but he who sows to the Spirit
will of the Spirit reap everlasting life.

GALATIANS 6:8 NKJV

Show Me your hand. I have fashioned it to bring glory to
My Name. For My Name is above every Name, and praise and
glory belong to Me, and in Me every living thing shall rejoice.
For I will cause a light to shine out of the darkness, and in
that place where you have walked in defeat, there I will cause
victory to break forth.

Rise, arise, and put on your strength, for you are a people
called by My Name, and in My Name you will be strong and
accomplish great things. And I will bless you out of the abundance of heaven.

My strength shall be your delivering power.

Where have I walked in defeat?

Holiness upon the Heart

from *On the Highroad of Surrender*

Just as He chose us in Him before the foundation of the world,
that we should be holy and without blame before Him in love.

EPHESIANS 1:4 NKJV

I the Lord have tried you. I have placed in your path the
open pit. I have given you the freedom to choose either good
or evil. Be not deceived. Though you see no eye, you are being
looked upon, and though you seek no voice, I continue to call.

I have entreated in love and chastened you in pity. Turn to
Me, My child. Open your heart to My grace.

Holiness shall be written upon the hearts of My people.
They shall minister in power because they live in obedience,
and if any do not desire obedience and discipline, he shall not
be My disciple.

How open is my heart to God's grace?

Soul's Rest

from *Come Away My Beloved*

And [God] hath raised us up together, and made us sit
together in heavenly places in Christ Jesus.

EPHESIANS 2:6

*B*ring Me all that puzzles you. Many questions need no answer, for when the heart is at one with the Father, there comes
an illumination of Spirit that transcends thought.

Learn to worship and you will have rest of soul; you will
rise to a new place of fellowship, where you will be made to
"sit together in heavenly places in Christ Jesus."

You will be taught by the Spirit. Yes, He will open the mysteries of the Word to you. For it was by the Spirit of God that
the scriptures were given to holy men of old; even so, by the
Spirit will the treasures of the Word be revealed to you.

How often do I hear the Spirit's voice?

Folly of Immaturity

from *On the Highroad of Surrender*

And that you put on the new man which was created
according to God, in righteousness and true holiness.

EPHESIANS 4:24 NKJV

---

*I*t is so simple when you approach Me in proper fashion
and do not hinder your spiritual progress by regression to a
parent-child position in your attitude. I know full well when
you are no longer properly in that stage, and although you
may attempt to fall back into it to avoid responsibility, I will
not respond, and you will be left to a folly of your own making.

When have I fallen into immaturity?

The Importance of Time and Kindness

from *Progress of Another Pilgrim*

Be ye therefore followers of God, as dear children;
and walk in love, as Christ also hath loved us,
and hath given himself for us an offering and a
sacrifice to God for a sweetsmelling savour.

EPHESIANS 5:1-2

Time is of supreme importance. Waste none. Let Me help you know what is worthy of attention and what is not; otherwise, you may be tempted to eliminate the things I most desire you to do.

Having a schedule will help you, but remember that kindness is more indicative of spiritual fervor than all your efficiency in work. Never let your works of righteousness crowd out the little acts of thoughtfulness. The labors of the hands must never take precedence over the gentle expressions of a compassionate heart.

Am I both righteous and thoughtful?

Speak the Truth

from *Come Away My Beloved*

Finally, my brethren, be strong in the Lord,
and in the power of his might.

EPHESIANS 6:10

*D*o not be intimidated by anyone, but speak forth My Word
as I give it to you.

You are not pleasing Me but trying to please men. They will
detect your inconsistency in spite of your best efforts, for in
one way or another, the truth will break through. You need
not say all that is in your heart, but you must either speak the
truth or be silent. If you cannot bring yourself to speak the
truth without apology, then speak nothing.

Let the life and witness of Jesus Christ be your guide.

Am I speaking the truth without apology?

The Mystery of Righteousness

from *On the Highroad of Surrender*

For we do not wrestle against flesh and blood, but against principalities, against powers, against the rulers of the darkness of this age, against spiritual hosts of wickedness in the heavenly places.

EPHESIANS 6:12 NKJV

*G*race is My abundant mercies showered upon the spiritually destitute. It is the fullness of My love poured out upon the loveless. Return unto Me, and I will forgive your iniquities and heal your backslidings.

There is no peace in the heart of the transgressor and no joy in his spirit. But though you leave Me, I have not left you. With your own hands you have made for your soul a shack. I have prepared for you a mansion. You have chosen death, but I have chosen for you life in its abundance.

Do not faint, My child, and do not forsake the way of the Spirit for the way of the flesh.

What backslidings do I need to confess?

Concentration

from *On the Highroad of Surrender*

For we do not wrestle against flesh and blood,
but against principalities, against powers, against the
rulers of the darkness of this age, against spiritual hosts
of wickedness in the heavenly places.

EPHESIANS 6:12 NKJV

Give your full strength to the conflict. Think of nothing else. Only concentration brings results. Lo, the enemy is concentrating against you to destroy you. You will have to bring a stronger force to bear against him if you hope to escape, much less defeat him.

Gird on your armor, for the battle is not against flesh and blood, but against principalities and powers and against spiritual forces of darkness intruding into sacred places. I am at your side to help you.

What spiritual battles am I currently facing?

The Power of Holiness

from *On the Highroad of Surrender*

For we do not wrestle against flesh and blood,
but against principalities, against powers,
against the rulers of the darkness of this age, against
spiritual hosts of wickedness in the heavenly places.

EPHESIANS 6:12 NKJV

❧

*T*he devil does not seek to destroy the vile person so much as the holy one. All hell trembles when God's prophet takes command in the Name of Jesus over evil powers. This is the man who is hated by the adversary. But though all hell should rise against him, I will give My servant power to stand, and he shall know that his own soul is being preserved by the very power of holiness within him, which is My own Spirit, the true objective of the enemy.

Is it not written that "He who is with you is greater than he who is in the world"?

What evil can I battle in Jesus' name?

Courage

from *Come Away My Beloved*

And take the helmet of salvation, and the sword
of the Spirit, which is the word of God.

EPHESIANS 6:17

———•—•———•—•———•—•———

$\mathcal{M}$y people shall not go mourning, for I the Lord will be
their rejoicing and their song. They will not be a complaining
people, for I will take away the murmuring from your streets.
Will I lead into the battlefronts an army of weeping women?
Will I ask the fainthearted to war? No, but I shall give My
people brave and courageous spirits, and I will make them
strong of heart. I will give them the spirit of the martyrs, for
they will be My witnesses of resurrection power. They shall be
stalwart. They shall be steadfast.

So take upon you the full armor of God.

Have I put on His full armor?

Perseverance, the Angel of Love

from *On the Highroad of Surrender*

Praying always with all prayer and supplication in the Spirit,
being watchful to this end with all perseverance
and supplication for all the saints.

EPHESIANS 6:18 NKJV

Perseverance is the rope that ties the soul to the doorpost of heaven. Without it even the most pious will fail. With it, the most stupid attain.

Not to give up in face of the impossible is humanity's ultimate salvation. It is well called "the perseverance of the saints," for it requires saintly determination to continue on in dedication when all the forces of hell are arrayed against the soul.

Perseverance is to the human spirit what the rudder is to a ship. It will steer the ship dead ahead in spite of the contrary wind.

This you must have, My child. . .not fleshly zeal, but holy determination, pressing on in defiance of all odds.

How is my perseverance?

My Words Cannot Wait

from *On the Highroad of Surrender*

Being confident of this very thing,
that He who has begun a good work in you
will complete it until the day of Jesus Christ.

PHILIPPIANS 1:6 NKJV

The hour is late, and the time for ministering is limited. Delay not, but hasten to finish the work. Do that which is nearest at hand. I shall open a way for its fulfillment, so you need not hold back, wondering how the provisions will be supplied. Lacked you ever in the past? Have you not acted in each case with faith in Me as your only hope?

My words cannot wait, but you have held them as though you thought the future would wait. Up! Delay no more. Obey Me, and do so quickly. Look directly to Me. I will empower and I will make all things possible as you move in obedience.

Who should I minister to today?

The Call of the Spirit

from *On the Highroad of Surrender*

Therefore, my beloved, as you have always obeyed, not as in
my presence only, but now much more in my absence, work
out your own salvation with fear and trembling; for it is God
who works in you both to will and to do for His good pleasure.

PHILIPPIANS 2:12–13 NKJV

*T*oday is the day of salvation. Tomorrow is not given you to
possess. Tomorrow is not a mysterious unknown: it will be
the fruit of what you sow today. Your response to Me at this
moment becomes your present experience of salvation. Your
answer to My call at the point where you now find yourself is
the one deciding factor.

Regret weakens, and procrastination destroys the vision.

Repent. With a whole heart seek My face and My forgiveness. Grace will be given according to the depth of your confession of need.

What needs do I need to confess to God today?

Salvation

from *Progress of Another Pilgrim*

Wherefore, my beloved, as ye have always obeyed,
not as in my presence only, but now much more in my
absence, work out your own salvation with fear and
trembling. For it is God which worketh in you both
to will and to do of his good pleasure.

PHILIPPIANS 2:12-13

*W*ork out your own salvation, says the scripture, for it is
God who "worketh in you both to will and to do of His good
pleasure." Thus, when you are conscious of spiritual weakness, do not wait for Me to move upon you to effect a change
from without, but assume the responsibility for your weakened condition as though you were indeed your own savior. In
the self-same moment, My grace will do the rest!

Wholeness is the product of the Spirit, but it cannot come
until your own desire sets it in motion.

How am I working out my salvation?

Vision Versus Dreams

from *On the Highroad of Surrender*

But indeed I also count all things loss for the excellence
of the knowledge of Christ Jesus my Lord, for whom
I have suffered the loss of all things, and count
them as rubbish, that I may gain Christ.

PHILIPPIANS 3:8 NKJV

*N*o sacrifice should be looked upon as such if it is made for
My glory. You shall suffer and forget, and sacrifice with no
thought of the price. My blessing should be of more value to
you than all your possessions, and yes, even more than your
aspirations and ideals, for these are still expressions of the
desire of the ego for fulfillment.

In My Spirit there can be no cherishing of personal dreams.
Only the doing of the Father's will is to be sought, and there is
a vast difference between a God-inspired vision and personal
dreams and aspirations.

Do I have visions or dreams?

Forewarned and Forearmed

from *On the Highroad of Surrender*

Not that I have already attained, or am already perfected;
but I press on, that I may lay hold of that for which
Christ Jesus has also laid hold of me.

PHILIPPIANS 3:12 NKJV

*N*ever waver once you have clear guidance. If you set out to do what I have bidden and sudden fear grips your heart, know that it is a device of the enemy. I am not the author of fear but of courage and a settled mind.

Confusion is the dust raised by the feet of the devil, calculated to cloud your vision and blind your eyes to the good I have placed directly in your path, and which you will surely find if you continue to act in faith.

Am I wavering or standing firm in Jesus?

Communication

from *Progress of Another Pilgrim*

Brethren, I count not myself to have apprehended: but this
one thing I do, forgetting those things which are behind,
and reaching forth unto those things which are before,
I press toward the mark for the prize of the high calling
of God in Christ Jesus.

PHILIPPIANS 3:13-14

*K*eep in vital communication with Me. Loose yourself from
the world at every possible point. You can fulfill My purpose
only when your channel is completely open and free to Me.
Resist every hindrance. Yield to Me the deepest place in your
consciousness. Only in this way do I have full control of your
life energies. Otherwise, you dissipate them in ignorance,
unintentionally. I will preserve them for the Spirit's activity
as you abide in the place of communion.

Do not look for any other secret of spiritual power. There is
none.

How can I keep that vital line of communication open?

Press On

from *On the Highroad of Surrender*

I press toward the goal for the prize of
the upward call of God in Christ Jesus.

PHILIPPIANS 3:14 NKJV

My child, you have crossed a bridge. Reach not back. Move
on ahead and press into the fullness of all I have prepared for
you. It is the blossoming of that which long ago was planted
and for many years has been nurtured. It is waiting for you to
step forward and receive. Do not tarry, and do not question,
neither allow doubts to enter your mind. Your heart may cry
out and rebel, but if you will turn to Me in those moments, I
will give you My peace. I send you no place except as I have
gone before.

Where is God sending me?

Ministering Angels

from *Come Away My Beloved*

Be anxious for nothing, but in everything by prayer
and supplication, with thanksgiving,
let your requests be made known to God.

PHILIPPIANS 4:6 NKJV

*B*e anxious for nothing. It is enough that I love you. I take
thought of your smallest need. Surely I will not allow you to be
put to shame and will not be unconcerned when you are in any
kind of need.

Always turn to Me before you look to any other source of
assistance. My love will light your path, so that you may be
guided in finding other help. I have given you ministering
angels, who may sometimes come to you in the form of your
friends. Accept their help as from Me, and your blessing will
be doubled. You may also, in turn, be used in similar manner
to bless others.

What "other source of assistance" am I tempted to turn to?

You Shall Move Swiftly

from *Come Away My Beloved*

Be anxious for nothing, but in everything by
prayer and supplication, with thanksgiving,
let your requests be made known to God.

PHILIPPIANS 4:6 NKJV

I will make My will known to you, and you will no longer
move haltingly; you shall move swiftly and surely. You may
not know what I am doing as yet, but you will know hereafter,
and you will be moved by My divine unction and authority.

You will not be left to falter as a blind man searches out his
way; with your hand in Mine, we will move together. My Spirit
will be apparent by your life and testimony, and you will be
empowered by My might and power.

Be anxious for nothing, but in all situations in prayer and
in fasting, bring each emergency case to Me, for I am the
Great Physician.

How swiftly do I move to do His will?

Hesitation

from *On the Highroad of Surrender*

I can do all things through Christ
who strengthens me.

PHILIPPIANS 4:13 NKJV

Never delay My blessing by indecision. I can only fill that which you give Me. If you do not act in response to My directives, you will never receive My enablement.

I give you strength according to the task, but I give it as you do the work. To hesitate is to become still more weak and timid, for it is a sense of inadequacy that causes you to draw back and fear to move, and this draws your attention to yourself. And because there is never sufficient power within yourself to do the Father's work, any focus on your own strength or ability will soon persuade you that the task is impossible.

Am I doing the work God called me to?

Provision

from *On the Highroad of Surrender*

And my God shall supply all your need according
to His riches in glory by Christ Jesus.

PHILIPPIANS 4:19 NKJV

*M*y promises wait their fulfillment in the lives of My
children. So much I would give. . .so little is received. Why live
so beggarly when the riches of heaven are yours for the ask-
ing? Having learned to receive from Me, you will find it easy
to give to all others, for you shall have no fear of lack, and no
need to guard your supply. Having found the source, you shall
never want.

David's heart was freed to sing, "The Lord is my shepherd,"
having come to know Him as his provider. Rejoice, My children, and walk in the freedom of My abundance, looking not
to others, but to Me for all things.

How easy is it for me to give to others?

Good and Evil

from *On the Highroad of Surrender*

That you may walk worthy of the Lord, fully pleasing
Him, being fruitful in every good work and
increasing in the knowledge of God.

COLOSSIANS 1:10 NKJV

*E*very foot of ground where you tread, that will I give you.
Walk in faith, and I will reward you with an abundance of
fruit.

It is not in your heart to discern your own way. Much that
is evil you call good, and much that is good you curse because
you will bless what you enjoy and condemn what gives you
displeasure.

I say unto you, My hand does not always deal joy. Joy may
come in the end, but the initial action may bring pain. Fear
not. I am not only wise but kind, and today's grief may become
the channel for tomorrow's blessing.

What blessings may come of today's griefs?

Sufferings Ahead

from *Come Away My Beloved*

Who now rejoice in my sufferings for you,
and fill up that which is behind of the afflictions of Christ
in my flesh for his body's sake, which is the church.

COLOSSIANS 1:24

*T*here are sufferings yet to be accomplished in the body of the Church that I was not able to suffer on the cross. Be patient, hold steady through the days that lie ahead, and know that the trials and suffering are working toward a consuming glory.

Praise Me out of a heart full of love. Praise Me for every blessing and every victory. Yes, praise Me when the most difficult thing to do is to praise. This is the victory that overcomes the world, even your faith, and praise is the voice of faith.

How steady am I in suffering?

Tribulation and Stamina

from *Make Haste My Beloved*

To whom God would make known what is the riches
of the glory of this mystery among the Gentiles;
which is Christ in you, the hope of glory.

COLOSSIANS 1:27

*O*nly through much prayer can you endure much tribulation.
In no other way can the new life in Christ develop and gain
stamina.

Be as a child and trust Me implicitly. I will honor your faith
and will give you still more.

Do not place restrictions on divine aid by trying to live the
Christian life in your own strength. I Myself am your victory.
My kingdom shall be forever, but even now it is in your heart
whenever you bow to Me as sovereign.

Is Christ truly my victory?

Take the Glory with You

from *Come Away My Beloved*

Not holding fast to the Head, from whom all the body,
nourished and knit together by joints and ligaments,
grows with the increase which is from God.

COLOSSIANS 2:19 NKJV

---

*B*ehold, I have brought you out of a dark and solitary land. I
have given you a drink from My own hand. We have held sweet
counsel together, for I have not called you servant, but I have
called you friend. Yes, and I delight in your companionship.
For I have seen your devotion, and I have observed with pleasure your thoughtfulness to those less fortunate who have
crossed your path.

Take the glory of the mountaintop with you; take My presence, My light, My love. This is not the valley of personal darkness—this is the valley where you will find those who need the
touch of blessing you can bring.

How am I sharing that touch of blessing?

Fight Discouragement

from *Progress of Another Pilgrim*

If ye then be risen with Christ, seek those things which are above, where Christ sitteth on the right hand of God. Set your affection on things above, not on things on the earth.

COLOSSIANS 3:1–2

*M*y son, turn not from the path of truth. Many testings shall beset you, but your God shall be your refuge.

Open wide your soul, and the Lord will fill it with His goodness. Your heart shall drink in His mercy and love, for His ear is attuned to your cry, and your desire toward Him shall be generously rewarded.

He knows your need and the depth of your searching. Only as you fight discouragement can you make room for Him to bless you in full measure as He desires to do.

How can I fight discouragement?

Your Life Is as a Weaving

from *Come Away My Beloved*

Let the peace of God rule in your hearts.

COLOSSIANS 3:15

*M*y child, your life is as a weaving. Beauty will not come to you by joy alone. Life may be tortuous and the pathway rough. From fabrics of lovely silk and from cords of rougher materials, I fashion what pleases Me. You may never know why certain experiences come. It is enough that My hand brings them all.

My grace is not limited by sorrow and difficulty. Indeed, it shines like a strand of gold mixed in with the black of grief. My hand moves with infinite love, and I am creating a pattern of intricate beauty.

Never be dismayed. The end will bring rejoicing for both yourself and Me. For you are My workmanship, created in Christ, even in His mind before the worlds existed.

What is God working in my life?

Words of Healing

from *Progress of Another Pilgrim*

Let the word of Christ dwell in you richly in all wisdom;
teaching and admonishing one another in psalms
and hymns and spiritual songs, singing with
grace in your hearts to the Lord.

COLOSSIANS 3:16

Speak evil of no man, but conceal the evil by speaking that
which is good. (Love covers a multitude of sins, and it is the
glory of love to conceal a matter.) In so doing you will heal, not
wound. You desire to have a healing ministry. Let it embrace
both the body and the soul, and be not content to heal bodies
while wounding souls.

Learn to minister blessing and comfort to the spirit
through your words and thus enhance the ministry of physical healing.

How can I minister blessing and comfort?

The Bent of the Soul

from *On the Highroad of Surrender*

And whatever you do in word or deed, do all in the name of the
Lord Jesus, giving thanks to God the Father through Him.

COLOSSIANS 3:17 NKJV

I am in the midst of sorrow and joy alike. I am in business
as surely as I am in the sanctuary of worship. In fact, the former becomes the proving ground of the latter. Be content in
all places and be at ease in your spirit.

In tests you are made strong. Do not run from them in
search of Me.

Your own inner consecration hallows the outer action.
Two may do what appears to be the same work. To one it is
holy and to the other it is carnal. The difference is in the
bent of the soul. . .whether it be for the glory of God or for
self-aggrandizement. I breathe My very life into that which is
offered to Me as a sacrifice of love.

Do I do all to His glory?

The Prophet's Tongue

from *Make Haste My Beloved*

Let your speech be always with grace, seasoned with salt,
that ye may know how ye ought to answer every man.

COLOSSIANS 4:6

*N*o prophet of Mine is worthy of the name who brings
reproach upon Zion by a careless tongue. He who speaks My
words at any time must guard his lips at all times. He is an
unworthy mouthpiece who delivers My message in one breath
and denies Me in a selfish moment by words that offend My
Spirit.

What is my tongue seasoned with?

Praise Transforms

from *On the Highroad of Surrender*

In everything give thanks; for this is
the will of God in Christ Jesus for you.

1 THESSALONIANS 5:18 NKJV

*R*ejoice in Me always, for as you rejoice and give thanks,
you release heaven's treasures and shower upon your head
the blessings of a delighted Father. Nothing so thoroughly
delights the Father's heart as the praises of His children.

For praise inclines the heart toward gratitude, and gratitude nurtures contentment, and you may know for a certainty
that no fruit ever appears on the tree of discontent.

So praise, My children, and never cease in your praising, for
in the midst of it I will manifest Myself, and you will understand that when I demand of you your praises, it is for your
highest good.

Praise will transform the humblest dwelling to a hallowed
haven.

How can I praise God today?

Adversity

from *Progress of Another Pilgrim*

In every thing give thanks: for this is the
will of God in Christ Jesus concerning you.

1 THESSALONIANS 5:18

*T*here are no calamities that do not work for your blessing when your heart is directed toward Me. When you do not
strive against adversity, its power to hurt you is destroyed.
The flesh may suffer, but the spirit will be blessed.

My voice speaks through every situation to the ear that is
yielded to the Spirit. My love flows freely through every sorrow
to the heart that is devoted to Me. I will not fail anyone—ever, so
long as that one is resting and trusting in My goodness.

Evils pass as ships in the night when peace reigns in the
surrendered soul. Leave with Me every unsolved problem.
Praise Me, and rejoice while I work it all out for My glory.

What unsolved problems can I leave with the Lord?

I Require More

from *Progress of Another Pilgrim*

And the very God of peace sanctify you wholly; and I pray
God your whole spirit and soul and body be preserved
blameless unto the coming of our Lord Jesus Christ.
Faithful is he that calleth you, who also will do it.

1 THESSALONIANS 5:23-24

*S*trive to be perfectly yielded to the Holy Spirit. He will do
much for you beyond what has been done in you up to this
point. You have truly given Me much in the past, but I require
more now because of the ministry I have for you to accomplish.

Let Me work in you with full liberty. You cannot do it yourself. I am the sanctifier. Only give Me the freedom to work.
You will be amazed at how easily it can be done.

How much freedom have I given God to work in my life?

Set Your Course by My Promises

from *Come Away My Beloved*

The Lord is faithful, who will establish
you and guard you from the evil one.

2 THESSALONIANS 3:3 NKJV

*B*e not afraid. I will not allow your adversaries to swallow
you up. You are My child; I will deliver you, honor you, and be
glorified through you. Because of My faithfulness to you, even
your enemies will recognize My power. Hold to My promises.
They are given to you as a chart is given to a ship, and a compass to the hunter. You may set your course and find your way
by My promises. They will lead you and guide you in places
where there is no trodden path.

Study My Word. It abounds with nuggets of courage. It
will strengthen you and help you, and even in eternity you
will partake of its far-reaching effects.

How much do God's promises chart my course?

Eternal Destiny of the Present Moment

from *Come Away My Beloved*

Be an example to the believers in word, in conduct,
in love, in spirit, in faith, in purity.

1 TIMOTHY 4:12 NKJV

*My child, it is not appointed to you to know the future. It is enough that we should walk together in love and trust. No doubts need mar your peace. Rest in the knowledge that My ways are perfect and My grace is all-sufficient. My help is adequate, no matter what may befall you.

Let no one say to you, "This will be, or that will surely come to pass." Live, rather, in the awareness of the eternal destiny of the present moment. To be unduly occupied with matters of the future is to your own disadvantage. So much is waiting to be done now.

Am I sensing the eternal destiny of the present moment?

Be Not Negligent

from *Progress of Another Pilgrim*

Wherefore I put thee in remembrance that thou stir up the
gift of God, which is in thee by the putting on of my hands.

2 TIMOTHY 1:6

*B*e not negligent concerning the gift I have given you. Do
not allow it to become dormant. I have given it to you knowing full well the urgency of this hour. Be up and about your
Father's business. Let nothing else claim priority over this,
My commission to you.

You shall suffer loss, and not you alone but multitudes
of others, if indolence overtakes you. My people are searching for food, and the pastures are sparse. There is need for
the provision of nourishment. Yes, My Body must be fed and
cared for and supplied the necessary nutriments for health
and growth.

Am I negligent or industrious about my Father's business?

Eternal Values

from *Progress of Another Pilgrim*

For the which cause I also suffer these things:
nevertheless I am not ashamed: for I know whom
I have believed, and am persuaded that he is
able to keep that which I have committed
unto him against that day.

2 TIMOTHY 1:12

*E*very motion in your life becomes impregnated with sublime significance as you are wholly dedicated to Me. All of time becomes charged with eternal values as it is consecrated and given to Me.

How dedicated am I to God?

Release the Blessings Also

from *Progress of Another Pilgrim*

That good thing which was committed unto thee
keep by the Holy Ghost which dwelleth in us.

2 TIMOTHY 1:14

———◦─╂─◦———◦─╂─◦———◦─╂─◦———

*Y*ou are accustomed to give Me liberty to take from you all
that is displeasing to Me. Now I ask that you give Me daily
all that blesses. I will bless it and protect it and safeguard it
for you.

All rest of heart comes through committal. You have been
taught to release your burdens. Part of your anxiety at this
moment has come from a feeling of responsibility to the care
of that priceless thing which I Myself have given you. So I say:
Give it to Me! I will not *take* it from you, but I will *keep* it for
you, and thus it shall be twice blessed.

Let Me guard your treasure.

What blessings do I need to release back to God?

Triumphs Rise Out of Defeats

from *Progress of Another Pilgrim*

If we suffer, we shall also reign with him:
if we deny him, he also will deny us.

2 TIMOTHY 2:12

---

*B*e patient as My hand deals with you. Blessings are born out of pain. Triumphs rise out of the dust of defeats when the defeats are offered up to Me and you go on again in faith.

Never despair.

When have I trusted my defeats to God's hand?

Preparation

from *Progress of Another Pilgrim*

Study to shew thyself approved unto God, a workman that
needeth not to be ashamed, rightly dividing the word of truth.

2 TIMOTHY 2:15

*M*y child, I would speak to you as to a disciple. What is
in your hand? Would you attempt to do a work with broken
instrument? You desire to serve Me in many ways. Have you
carefully prepared? Or do you expect Me to overrule your lack
of wisdom? Lo, I say unto you, preparation is your own responsibility. Certainly I will help you in it, but I am not glorified
through a vessel that is careless concerning its condition.

How well prepared am I to serve God?

Useless Striving

from *Make Haste My Beloved*

The servant of God must not strive.

2 TIMOTHY 2:24

*B*e careful that you are following Me, and I will care for all else. Striving is for those who have not yet learned to trust Me. Anxiety is the affliction of the self-possessed. The godly know their heritage and revel in the protection of their Redeemer. For it is in the blood of Jesus that refuge is found for every onslaught of the enemy.

What is my spiritual heritage?

A Perpetual Fountain of Glory

from *Come Away My Beloved*

I have fought the good fight, I have finished the race,
I have kept the faith.

2 TIMOTHY 4:7 NKJV

*W*rite those things I say to you. Hold back nothing of all I shall say to you. For I shall speak to you in the darkness and shall make your way a path of light. I will cry to you out of the confusion round about, and you shall hear My voice and shall know that which I do.

Look to Me, and I will be your beacon in the night, and you will not stumble over the hidden things. You will walk in a way of victory though turmoil is on either hand, even as Israel marched through the Red Sea on a path My hand hewed out for them.

Am I looking only to Jesus?

Dependence on God

from *Come Away My Beloved*

For we have become partakers of Christ if
we hold the beginning of our confidence
steadfast to the end.

HEBREWS 3:14 NKJV

Do not walk carelessly, nor lay out your own paths on
which to travel. You cannot know what lies in the distance.
So walk closely with Me, that you may be able to draw quickly
upon My aid. You need Me, and no matter how well-developed
your faith is or how mature is your growth in grace, never
think for a moment that you need My support any less. The
truth is that you need it even more. For I shelter the newborn
from many of the trials and tests I permit to confront those
who are growing up in spiritual stature.

Move forward with courage and confidence, but always
allow Me to walk ahead, and choose the right path.

When have I walked behind Jesus?

Discover the Power of Truth

from *Progress of Another Pilgrim*

For the word of God is quick, and powerful, and sharper than
any twoedged sword, piercing even to the dividing asunder
of soul and spirit, and of the joints and marrow, and is a
discerner of the thoughts and intents of the heart.

HEBREWS 4:12

Discover the power of Truth—any truth. Put it to the test.
Every truth is as firm as I am. It can be relied upon. It can be
trusted as a fact and counted upon in experience.

Believe My truths, but go beyond this. Put them into operation, and learn what it is to experience them as well. Only in
this way can you proclaim their fact in a persuasive manner.
No teaching is effective except as it springs out of experience,
and no teaching which does spring from experience shall fall
short.

*Which of God's truths do I need to put
into operation in my life?*

Total Relinquishment

from *Progress of Another Pilgrim*

For we have not an high priest which cannot be touched
with the feeling of our infirmities; but was in all
points tempted like as we are, yet without sin.

HEBREWS 4:15

As you ponder the sufferings of the Lord Jesus Christ, you shall gain insight into your own pain. That which is of the Spirit must be discerned in the Spirit. Only in prayer and meditation on the Holy Word can understanding come to your heart, and only thus can you be truly comforted in the depth of the spirit where the suffering occurs.

Nothing can remain of self-will if My full purpose is to be accomplished. Slowly, unrelentingly, each soul moves to his own Gethsemane of total relinquishment of all his cherished personal hopes and on to his own barren Golgotha.

When has my self-will limited God's purpose in my life?

The Singing Heart

from *On the Highroad of Surrender*

Now faith is the substance of things hoped for,
the evidence of things not seen.

HEBREWS 11:1

*P*atience, My child, will manifest where hope is nurtured.
The singing heart is blind to obstacles and recognizes in all
things the loving hand of an all-wise Father. In such a state,
delays are unnoticed, for the Spirit is not bound by the limitations of outer circumstances. The power of evil to destroy joy
is nullified when Christ Himself becomes the one point of attention. In Him all things are possessed now, for faith beholds
that which is yet to be as though it were already a reality.

Withdraw your attention from the outer circumstance
and lose yourself, My child, in the free-flowing stream of the
Spirit.

What "outer circumstances" do I need to look past today?

Sincerity

from *Come Away My Beloved*

But without faith it is impossible to please Him, for he
who comes to God must believe that He is, and that He is a
rewarder of those who diligently seek Him.

HEBREWS 11:6 NKJV

*M*arvel not that I have said you must be born anew. Of the
flesh, nothing spiritual can ever be produced.

This is why I said I loathed your sacrifices. It was not that I
despised the ordinance in itself, but I perceived that it was an
expression of self-righteousness, showing your indifference
to the claim of God upon your heart.

My ordinances are good and holy, but they are to be entered
into with deep sincerity and with awareness of their true
significance. To sacrifice in carelessness and ignorance is to
damage your own soul. Let your spirit never become callous.

What is my heart attitude in sacrifice?

Run with Patience

from *Come Away My Beloved*

Wherefore seeing we also are compassed about with
so great a cloud of witnesses, let us lay aside every weight,
and the sin which doth so easily beset us, and let us run
with patience the race that is set before us.

HEBREWS 12:1

I could by adversity strip from you the comforts of life, but I
will bless you in double portion if, of your own accord, you do
as the apostle Paul and lay aside every weight, resisting the
many temptations that continually beset you as you run with
patience the course I set before you.

"Running" with "patience"—in these two words I have
combined the intensity of purpose and the quiet waiting upon
Me you must have, or else you will be overtaken in the race by
fatigue of body and soul.

How patiently am I running the race before me?

Hold Fast

from Come Away My Beloved

Looking unto Jesus, the author and finisher of our faith,
who for the joy that was set before Him endured the cross,
despising the shame, and has sat down at the
right hand of the throne of God.

HEBREWS 12:2 NKJV

*H*old fast that which you have, and let no one take your crown.

Let no one hinder you in pursuit of the reward.

Let nothing stand in the way of your complete victory.

Let no weariness or discouraging thought cause you to loosen
the rope of faith, but bind it tighter and anchor fast to My Word.

My Word can never fail.

Emmanuel! God with us!

Praise His holy, wonderful Name! For this He made us.

For this He destined us! For this He predestinated us!

For this He died and rose.

For this He sent that first mighty outpouring at Pentecost.

Praise God! Praise God!

What stands in the way of my complete victory?

The Art of Constancy

from *Progress of Another Pilgrim*

By him therefore let us offer the sacrifice
of praise to God continually, that is, the fruit
of our lips giving thanks to his name.

HEBREWS 13:15

*L*et nothing draw your attention away from Me. In the
midst of every legitimate activity, your soul can be focused
on Me if gratitude and adoration and worship have captured
your heart. The soul of a man may be a continual chapel of
praise as he learns the art of constancy in loving Me first and
foremost.

You frequently emphasize how much you should love Me.
This is important, but even more important to Me, and to you,
is the constancy of your love. . .that it be the overflowing grace
of your heart continually, so that every waking hour you are
truly and literally walking and worshipping in the Spirit.

How can worship overflow in my life?

Perfecting of Soul

from *Progress of Another Pilgrim*

Now the God of peace. . .make you perfect in every
good work to do his will, working in you that which is
wellpleasing in his sight, through Jesus Christ;
to whom be glory for ever and ever. Amen.

HEBREWS 13:20-21

If you set up barriers through pride or self-defense, you
hinder the progress of your soul. Be as a little child, and stay
open to the flow of My life in you: so shall you be spared many
a bitter disappointment and much weary striving. Only in
this way can you keep your balance and poise. Thus shall your
perfecting be accomplished.

Nothing you could ever do for Me can be more important
than this—the perfecting of your own soul.

How has pride hindered the progress of my soul?

Patience and Perfection

from *Progress of Another Pilgrim*

But let patience have her perfect work,
that ye may be perfect and entire, wanting nothing.

JAMES 1:4

---

*P*atience, My child, is not a matter of forethought nor self-control. It will manifest itself quite naturally and without effort when the soul is rid of all resentment against imperfection. Perfection is the goal toward which a man strives, but perfection is never attained as long as man is in his mortal body. Purity of heart is possible, in a measure, but perfection is a word that could have been used to describe only a few rare souls, and then only relatively.

The only way you can make any reasonable progress toward perfection is by committing your entire life into My hands and realizing it is I who live within you and effect whatever changes are made.

Is patience working in my life?

The Need for Greater Faith

from *Come Away My Beloved*

If any of you lacks wisdom, let him ask of God,
who gives to all liberally and without reproach,
and it will be given to him.

JAMES 1:5 NKJV

O child, do not expect the trials to be lighter than in the past.
Why should you think the tests would be less severe? I test
all things, and there are areas of your life that as yet I have
not touched. Do not look for respite. The days ahead may call
for greater endurance and more robust faith than you ever
needed before.

Apply your heart to learn wisdom. This goal transcends
every other aim, and any other good that comes out of a pressure period is an added blessing in excess.

Seek Me above all else.

How important to me is wisdom?

Tensions Build Fortitude

from *Progress of Another Pilgrim*

Blessed is the man that endureth temptation:
for when he is tried, he shall receive the crown of life,
which the Lord hath promised to them that love him.

JAMES 1:12

*M*any perplexities bring you closer to Me, for as you seek
wisdom and need courage, you are driven to Me for help.
These are the times you become pliable in My hands. It is
the moment of crisis that reveals either a man's strength or
his weakness. It is the tension of life that builds fortitude or
exposes fear.

Know that I keep you, that I love you, that I fully understand.
Cast yourself wholly upon My mercy. Pray, knowing that the
request is already granted and the help already provided.

Act in faith: it is the secret of every victory.

When has tension pushed me nearer to God?

Love and Vain Religion

from *Make Haste My Beloved*

Pure religion and undefiled before God and the Father is this,
To visit the fatherless and widows in their affliction, and to
keep himself unspotted from the world.

JAMES 1:27

*H*e who does not express love exposes the darkness of his
soul, though he be clothed with religion. This man's religion is
vain, wrote James, if he does not express his faith by kindness
and good deeds (James 1:26-27). He needs no man to condemn
him; he condemns himself by his failure to show consideration for the feelings of his brother. No amount of pious
platitudes can outweigh his guilt. He has appointed himself to
a high place and is scarcely fit for the lowest.

"But he that is greatest among you shall be your servant,"
said Jesus (Matthew 23:11).

Is my religion vain or pure?

Let Him Take the Initiative

from *Progress of Another Pilgrim*

Submit yourselves therefore to God.

JAMES 4:7

*L*et no selfish motives rule your actions. Be motivated by the love of God, and if you truly are, you can rest assured that whatever you do has the approval of your Father.

You cannot do with joy some of the things that may be permissible for another. You are not free to make your own choices as long as you are surrendered to the Will of God, for when you are yielded to Him, it is He who gives the directions. Wait for Him to take the initiative.

When have I let God take the initiative in my life?

Heart-Purity

Therefore submit to God. Resist the devil and he will flee from you. Draw near to God and He will draw near to you.

JAMES 4:7–8 NKJV

*M*y children, it is not by grieving over your sins that they are forgiven. My forgiveness is in constant operation and you need only accept it. The cleansing of your heart and the restoration of your joy depends upon your full confession and willingness to repent and to renounce your sin. Exercise your soul toward the achievement of heart-purity. Until this work is accomplished (and maintained) you will not have inner peace.

This unrest and conflict is not caused by My attitude toward you but by your attitude toward yourself. Seek My face in repentance until you have yielded to Me all that distresses you.

How do I view my own sins?

I Seek to Lift Your Load

from *Come Away My Beloved*

Humble yourselves in the sight of the Lord,
and He will lift you up.

JAMES 4:10 NKJV

Seek Me early; seek Me late; seek Me in the midst of the day. You need Me in the early hours for direction and guidance and for My blessing upon your heart. You need Me at the end of the day to commit into My hands the day's happenings—both to free yourself of the burdens and to give them over into My hands so I may continue to work things out. And you need Me more than ever in the busy hours, so that I may give you My grace and My tranquility and My wisdom.

I desire to take the tensions of life from you.

How humble am I before God?

Conviction and Forgiveness

from *Come Away My Beloved*

Confess your trespasses to one another, and pray for one
another, that you may be healed. The effective,
fervent prayer of a righteous man avails much.

JAMES 5:16 NKJV

My patience is running out. I have purposed and man has
despised. I have willed and you have resisted me. Do not be
smug in your own ways, for your ways are not My ways.

You are indulgent when I have called you to rigid discipline. You speak soft words when I would require you to speak
the truth. You interfere with the convicting work of My Holy
Spirit when you smooth over confession. I am not a severe
God, unmindful of the frailties of human nature, but I am a
God of divine love and holiness, and I desire your fellowship,
and I long for you to know My joy.

What do I need to confess?

Rely on My Faithfulness

from *Progress of Another Pilgrim*

[You] who are kept by the power of God through faith unto
salvation ready to be revealed in the last time.

1 PETER 1:5

*D*o not be anxious. My Spirit shall direct your steps. You
need have no fear. There is never a place where you walk that I
have not preceded you. There are many times when your faith
wavers. Take no account of it. I am keeping you even when you
do not feel strong. You must rely on My faithfulness—not on
your feelings.

Your strength will vary from day to day, but My power is
always available to you as you yield to the Holy Spirit.

Do I rely on His faithfulness or my feelings?

An Injection of New Life

from *Progress of Another Pilgrim*

Wherein ye greatly rejoice, though now for a season, if need
be, ye are in heaviness through manifold temptations.

1 PETER 1:6

All you do for Me in ministering to others is part of My
own working within you; for in every case, whenever you bless
another, you bring an injection of new life and vitality into
your own spirit and personality.

Your character is that which I shape from the broken frag-
ments of all your testings; therefore, accept the trials with a
grateful heart. I will use all things to bring you into conformity to My image if you will but bless all and trust Me.

How complete is my trust in God?

Testings

from *Progress of Another Pilgrim*

That the trial of your faith, being much more precious
than of gold that perisheth, though it be tried with fire,
might be found unto praise and honour and glory
at the appearing of Jesus Christ.

1 PETER 1:7

*I*n a multitude of testings I would perfect your understanding. I am not unaware of the pressures thus inflicted upon you, but as the trials come and go, I not only turn them into a means of blessing, but I never fail to make available My comfort and My sustaining strength.

How has God blessed me through trials?

The Headship of Christ

from *Progress of Another Pilgrim*

Wherefore gird up the loins of your mind, be sober,
and hope to the end for the grace that is to be brought
unto you at the revelation of Jesus Christ.

1 PETER 1:13

*M*any are looking to you for deliverance and for salvation. Be aware of every possible moment of opportunity. The destiny, yes, the eternal destiny of lives is at stake. A frivolous spirit or a careless indulgence in levity may rob both yourself and the other person of a priceless experience in the creative power of the Spirit of God. Don't take such a precarious path. Stay in the Spirit, and keep your mind in captivity to the mind and the thoughts of Christ. Be satisfied with nothing less. Anything less will cause you to be virtually unproductive.

Who might be looking to me for deliverance?

God's Mercy

from *Come Away My Beloved*

And above all things have fervent charity among yourselves:
for charity shall cover the multitude of sins.

1 PETER 4:8

If it is true that human love covers a multitude of sins,
how much more true is it of the divine love of God the Father!
Knowing My deep love for you, your own heart will no longer condemn you. My mercies are everlasting, My kindness,
abundant.

My grace extends to the least of My children, and My tenderness shall make you strong. I go before you daily to prepare your way, and you will be accompanied by My goodness
and My mercy.

When have I thanked God for His goodness and mercy?

Tribulation

from *On the Highroad of Surrender*

Beloved, do not think it strange concerning
the fiery trial which is to try you, as though
some strange thing happened to you.

1 PETER 4:12 NKJV

*T*hrough much tribulation I am bringing My chosen to perfection. Be not amazed when challenges present themselves. I am building your fortitude, and the day will come when you will be grateful for every lesson learned in the school of affliction.

How grateful am I for God's lessons in affliction?

I Shall Gather My People

from *Come Away My Beloved*

For the time has come for judgment to begin at the house
of God; and if it begins with us first, what will be the end
of those who do not obey the gospel of God?

1 PETER 4:17 NKJV

◦─┼◦──────◦┼◦──────◦┼─◦

*T*oday is the day of salvation (see 2 Corinthians 6:2), and
again: "Seek the Lord while He may be found" (Isaiah 55:6
NKJV), for the night comes. Then My wrath will be poured out
upon the ungodly, and there will be no hand stretched forth to
save.

Lift your eyes to the clouds, for the heavens are filled with
glory. Yes, He comes with ten thousand of His saints. Lift
your hearts, for you will not be afraid of those things that are
coming to pass upon the earth. For I shall gather My people to
Myself, and the flames will not touch them.

How do I feel about "those things that are coming to pass"?

A Rain of Fire

from *Make Haste My Beloved*

For the time is come that judgment must begin at the house of God: and if it first begin at us, what shall the end be of them that obey not the gospel of God?

1 PETER 4:17

My children, a rain of fire is falling, a rain of judgment upon My house. It is My people whom I am purifying now.

I shall send the fire as you wait upon Me. It shall bring you refreshment as a rain. It shall be death to the old carnal nature, but it shall be life to the inner man—the new nature that is yours in Christ.

Never be afraid of My judgments. I do not send them in wrath upon My church, but in love and compassion. Can I abandon you to your sin?

Can I see God's compassion in His judgments?

As Rains of Refreshing

from *Come Away My Beloved*

Humble yourselves therefore under the mighty
hand of God, that he may exalt you in due time.

1 PETER 5:6

O My beloved, do not be anxious concerning tomorrow. You
shall encounter nothing of which I am not already aware. My
mercy is concealed within every storm cloud. My grace flows
beneath every crosscurrent. My wisdom has conceived a solution to every perplexity.

I have deliberately set obstacles in your path to test your
prowess. The storm is not a thing to fear but rather to welcome. As soon as you have made the discovery that in the time
of stress and strain you have the clearest revelations of Myself, You will learn to head into the wind with sheer delight.

How do I view spiritual obstacles?

A Covert in the Storm

from *On the Highroad of Surrender*

Therefore humble yourselves under the mighty hand of God,
that He may exalt you in due time, casting all your
care upon Him, for He cares for you.

1 PETER 5:6-7 NKJV

*B*e at peace, My little one, for in Me there is a cover in the storm. My love remains changeless whatever winds may blow. My grace will sustain you however deep may be the night, however fierce may be the test.

Nothing harms the trusting soul though calamity be his companion. In affliction there shall be comfort, for he who abides in Me shall not know desolation. I protect, I provide, I enrich. None shall say in My presence, "I am poor," for he who loves Me is supremely blessed; My grace is his strength, and I am his salvation.

When have I found God's comfort in affliction?

Sincerity

from *Progress of Another Pilgrim*

Be sober, be vigilant; because your adversary the devil, as a
roaring lion, walketh about, seeking whom he may devour.

1 PETER 5:8

My child, be truly as a little child, and preserve within
your spirit the grace of simplicity. Maintain a candid honesty.
Resist all temptation to put on airs. Be natural. Strive to be
as Jesus, who was never pretentious, never evasive nor coy. Be
real, be sincere, for to serve God demands sincerity. The needs
of hearts and problems of life are real. Many carry burdens
and griefs, and how can you be of help in a frivolous state of
mind?

How sincere is my witness?

As a Lamb Before a Lion

from *Progress of Another Pilgrim*

Be sober, be vigilant; because your adversary the devil, as a
roaring lion, walketh about, seeking whom he may devour.

1 PETER 5:8

All kinds of dangers lurk about you. The enemy would rob
you of the most sacred blessing. He has no desire to take it
except to destroy it. Your power to protect it is no match for
his treachery. He lies in wait in the unexpected place, and you
are as a lamb before a lion.

At My feet leave all, and know it is for your ultimate joy.
Truly it is not a sacrifice. It will be your salvation.

What blessing have I left at God's feet?

Crisis Experiences

from *Progress of Another Pilgrim*

But the God of all grace, who hath called us unto his eternal
glory by Christ Jesus, after that ye have suffered a while,
make you perfect, stablish, strengthen, settle you.

1 PETER 5:10

I will never leave you alone in the midst of any affliction.
You cannot escape the crisis experiences if you desire to grow
and mature, but you need never fear them regardless of the
form they take, for My grace and My equanimity shall be as
a strong anchor that shall hold you fast, and you shall not be
driven off course.

When have I felt the tug of God's protecting anchor?

Repentance Activates My Grace

from *Progress of Another Pilgrim*

If we confess our sins, he is faithful and just to forgive us
our sins, and to cleanse us from all unrighteousness.
If we say that we have not sinned, we make him a liar,
and his word is not in us.

1 JOHN 1:9-10

Give Me all: your body, mind, and spirit. Hold nothing back
for yourself. Speak to Me often and much. The more you do so,
the more I can help you. Full confession brings full forgiveness. True humility opens the door to divine aid. Genuine
repentance activates My grace.

What sins do I need to confess to God?

Fresh Anointing

from Dialogues with God

And the world passeth away, and the lust thereof:
but he that doeth the will of God abideth for ever.

1 JOHN 2:17

*T*his is the doing of the will of God.

As it is written,

He that doeth the will of God abideth for ever. Service to Me by the will of the flesh is temporal, but the doing of the will of God is eternal.

And this is the will of God, that ye be about the Father's business—that ye work the works of Him that hath called thee and now sends thee, even as did Jesus when He walked among men.

Leave all else to Me.

Seek the fresh anointing and I will do the rest.

What is God's will for me today?

Not Lethargy but Surrender

from Progress of Another Pilgrim

And the world passeth away, and the lust thereof:
but he that doeth the will of God abideth for ever.

1 JOHN 2:17

You are called not to lethargy but surrender.

Happy is the man who puts his trust in the Lord, yes, even to the extent that he lets Him formulate the plans and direct the goings.

No reward is sweeter than to feel His commendation. No life is more tranquil than that lived in His will. At His feet there is peace. Turmoil shall not dwell in the home where Christ is the honored guest.

All of life becomes a hymn of praise when God's love rules the heart.

Is my life a hymn of praise?

Be Not Afraid of Solitude

from *Progress of Another Pilgrim*

But the anointing which ye have received of him abideth in
you, and ye need not that any man teach you: but as the same
anointing teacheth you of all things, and is truth, and is no
lie, and even as it hath taught you, ye shall abide in him.

1 JOHN 2:27

I have a ministry for you. You have not found it yet because
you have been earnestly and in sincerity and with humble
heart trying to conform to the patterns of others.

Be not afraid of solitude. You will not lose My touch. You
will not miss a blessing. How shall the hand of any other
bring you greater joy or clearer insight than I can bring to you
Myself?

Is there a ministry I need to seek His will on?

My Love Is Coexistent with My Power

from *Dialogues with God*

God is love; and he that dwelleth
in love dwelleth in God.

1 JOHN 4:16

—•••— ••— ••—

My child, I know thy frame and remember that thou art dust, for thus I fashioned thee. But is it not also written that I breathed upon man, and he became a living soul? Said I not that I made him in Mine own image and likeness? Yea, within the house of clay did I place a part of Myself. Without thee would My body be incomplete.

Draw near to My heart, for My love for thee is coexistent with My power. Yea, e'er thy face touch the dust, I have put Mine arms about thee to draw thee unto My heart.

When have I drawn near to His heart?

Identity

from *On the Highroad of Surrender*

We love Him because He first loved us. If someone says,
"I love God," and hates his brother, he is a liar;
for he who does not love his brother whom he has seen,
how can he love God whom he has not seen?

1 JOHN 4:19-20 NKJV

---

*O*ut of much tribulation I bring forth a people for the glory of
My Name. I am shaping you in the furnace of affliction that I
may set My seal upon you and display in you My own identity.
I desire that you be one with Me in all I have purposed.

My heart is grieved when those who profess to be My children neglect their intercessory prayer life. They do damage
to the spirit of grace when they neglect their responsibility
toward others. Can you love God while ignoring the need of
your brother?

Whom should I pray for today?

Physical Health and Spiritual Ministry

from *Progress of Another Pilgrim*

Beloved, I wish above all things that thou mayest prosper
and be in health, even as thy soul prospereth.

3 JOHN 1:2

*D*o not misconstrue the scripture which says "I beat my
body to keep it in subjection." A more clear way to state the
true intent would be to say, "By proper discipline and care of
the physical body, it may be made to fulfill the desires and
demands of the soul." Otherwise, you may, by lack of concern
for your physical health, hamper your spiritual ministry.

Run the race with a pure heart, and the reward shall be
given you. Your path is strewn with blessings. Enjoy them
fully and recognize that they are from My hand.

How do I discipline and care for my body?

Praying in the Spirit

from *Come Away My Beloved*

But you, beloved, building yourselves up on
your most holy faith, praying in the Holy Spirit,
keep yourselves in the love of God.

JUDE 20-21 NKJV

*A*s you set your soul through deliberate choice of your will
to worship Me by praying in the Spirit, you will find your faith
strengthened and your life bathed in My love.

With your faith laying hold on My promises and power, and
your actions motivated by My love, you will find yourself in
the path of My activity; My blessing shall be upon you, and I
will accomplish My works through you.

Am I praying in the Spirit?

Vital Contact

from *Progress of Another Pilgrim*

But ye, beloved, building up yourselves on your
most holy faith, praying in the Holy Ghost,
keep yourselves in the love of God, looking for the
mercy of our Lord Jesus Christ unto eternal life.

JUDE 20–21

*L*ive in constant communion with Me, and strive to maintain continual vital contact. So shall be generated within you the spiritual power which builds up a ready supply for the moments of actual ministry.

This is the reason Jesus spent long hours in lonely vigil with His Father. This is why the scriptures admonish you to pray without ceasing.

As you pray and meditate, you are enriched by the Spirit in the grace and compassion of Jesus Christ. Your soul is perfected as you kneel in His presence, even as a flower unfolds in the sunshine.

When can I make time for contact with God?

The Last Great Outpouring

from *Come Away My Beloved*

"I am the Alpha and the Omega, the Beginning
and the End," says the Lord, "who is and who
was and who is to come, the Almighty."

REVELATION 1:8 NKJV

———•✦•——— •✦• ———•✦•———

*Y*ou stand on the threshold of a new day. I have truly great things in store for you. I will bring to pass a new thing. You have heard of the showers, but I say to you: I will send a mighty downpour. In the day of the great deluge which is coming, many will come to know the reality of My power.

Surely I will pour out My Spirit. I will reaffirm the veracity of My Word and bring the message of the Gospel of Redemption to many who would otherwise never give heed. I am the Alpha and the Omega. Stand firm in Me. Never waver.

Am I standing firm, without wavering?

Warring in the Spirit

from *On the Highroad of Surrender*

And they overcame him by the blood of the
Lamb and by the word of their testimony,
and they did not love their lives to the death.

REVELATION 12:11 NKJV

*O*ut of many varied experiences the soul gains knowledge,
and knowledge brings strength and stability. It is vain to
battle spiritual elements with the carnal mind. Only the one
who is taught of the Spirit can war in the Spirit. You must war,
because there are enemies unseen to human eyes but constantly besieging the child of God. But he is not left defense-
less. Heavenly protection is his, as well as offensive weapons.
The sword of the Spirit, the blood of the Lamb, and the word of
testimony are provided for every saint of God, but must be put
into action in faith before they can bring about a deliverance.

How can I prepare for spiritual warfare?

My Kingdom Is at Hand

from *Come Away My Beloved*

Fear God and give glory to Him, for the hour of
His judgment has come; and worship Him who made
heaven and earth, the sea and springs of water.

REVELATION 14:7 NKJV

*B*y My Spirit, I will speak to My people. Those who hear My
voice will sing of My glory. Those who are pure of heart will
walk in a path of delight. Joy is the natural climate of heaven,
and My chosen ones will have a full portion even now.

Be prepared for Me, for I will come to you in blinding splen-
dor, and you will not be able to bear it if you have been regard-
ing the darkness about you. Look above the present scene, for
to dwell on the confusion of the world would render you unfit
for the revelation of heaven.

How prepared am I for the Lord's return?

Prepare Your Garments

from *Progress of Another Pilgrim*

And to her was granted that she should be
arrayed in fine linen, clean and white:
for the fine linen is the righteousness of saints.

REVELATION 19:8

---

*T*he day is at hand, and the Day Star riseth even now. You may not see Me yet, but I am only just beneath the rim of the horizon, and you shall behold Me shortly in all My glory.

How ought you to rise and make yourself ready! How you should put your house in order and prepare your garments!

Your garments shall be of fine linen, for it is the righteousness of the saints.

What can I do to prepare my garments?

Vivid Relationship

from *Dialogues with God*

Out of his mouth goeth a sharp sword, that with
it he should smite the nations: and he shall rule
them with a rod of iron: and he treadeth the winepress
of the fierceness and wrath of Almighty God.

REVELATION 19:15

*W*onderful Saviour! Blessed, holy sacrificial Lamb of God!
What depth of love Thou hast demonstrated for us through
Thy vicarious death on Calvary, and in Thy resurrection, what
sublime victory! What dynamic power was revealed in Thine
ascension, what promise of life to come, of ultimate triumph,
of complete deliverance from this present world, from suffering and shame—sin and death.

Lo, what great hope is set before us! Yea, what glory—what
rapture—what a mighty deliverance—what victory! Let Satan
do his worst: Christ has overcome.

What trials in my life can Christ overcome?

No Separation

from *Come Away My Beloved*

And I saw a new heaven and a new earth:
for the first heaven and the first earth were
passed away; and there was no more sea.

REVELATION 21:1

---

*H*e has stretched forth His mighty hand
  And has smitten the waters:
  He has made me to pass through dry-shod. Hallelujah! For
there will be no more sea.
  There will be no more separation!
  He has removed every barrier; He has bridged the gulf. He
has drawn me unto Himself, yes, into Himself.
  He has left the enemy in confusion and defeat.
  He has led me through the way of the wilderness,
  And His hand has been a shade from the burning heat.

When have I praised God for these blessings?

Scripture Index

OLD TESTAMENT

Genesis
1:31 . . . . .January 1
6:13-14 . . . . January 2
22:2 . . . . January 3
45:7 . . . . January 4
50:20 . . . . January 5

Exodus
12:23 . . . . January 6
20:3 . . . . January 7
33:18 . . . . January 8
40:38 . . . . January 9

Leviticus
6:21-22 . . . . January 10
18:4 . . . . .January 11

Numbers
13:30 . . . . January 12
14:24 . . . . January 13
32:23 . . . . January 14, January 15

Deuteronomy
5:12 . . . . January 16
8:16 . . . . January 17

Joshua
1:2 . . . . January 18
1:3 . . . . January 19
5:14 . . . . .January 20
14:14 . . . . January 21

Judges
7:7 . . . . January 22

Ruth
1:16 . . . . January 23

1 Samuel

1:11 . . . . January 24
17:36 . . . . January 25

2 Samuel

22:20 . . . . January 26
23:16 . . . . January 27

1 Kings

17:13 . . . . January 28
19:11 . . . . January 29

2 Kings

6:17 . . . . January 30

1 Chronicles

14:15 . . . . January 31

2 Chronicles

7:14 . . . . February 1
20:22 . . . . February 2

Nehemiah

4:18 . . . . February 3
9:21 . . . . February 4

Esther

2:12 . . . . February 5

Job

1:10 . . . . February 6
5:17-18 . . . . February 7
13:15 . . . . February 8
22:21 . . . . February 9
28:28 . . . . February 10

Psalms

16:1 . . . . .February 11
18:28-29 . . . . February 12
24:3-4 . . . . February 13
24:3-5 . . . . February 14
27:4 . . . . February 15
30:1-2 . . . . February 16
34:1 . . . . February 17
34:19 . . . . February 18

55:22 .... February 19
56:11 .... February 20
71:13-14 .... February 21
107:9 .... February 22
119:1-2 .... February 23
119:32 .... February 24
139:12 .... February 25
139:23-24 .... February 26

Proverbs

3:5 .... February 27
4:23 .... February 28
6:27 .... February 29
10:19 .... March 1
14:12 .... March 2
15:13 .... March 3
15:16 .... March 4
17:22 .... March 5
20:19 .... March 6
24:30-31 .... March 7
26:20 .... March 8
28:13 .... March 9
29:1 .... March 10

Ecclesiastes

11:1 .... March 11

Song of Solomon

1:15 .... March 12
2:10 .... March 13

Isaiah

1:19 .... March 14
6:8 .... March 15
26:3 .... March 16
30:15 .... March 17
32:17 .... March 18
32:18 .... March 19
33:6 .... March 20
35:7 .... March 21
40:31 .... March 22
41:17-18 .... March 23
43:2 .... March 24
45:2 .... March 25
48:10 .... March 26

48:17..March 27
53:3.. March 28
55:8.. March 29
55:11.. March 30
57:21..March 31
58:11.. April 1
59:19..April 2

Jeremiah
2:13 ....April 3
10:23..April 4
33:3..April 5

Lamentations
3:22–23..April 6

Ezekiel
1:16 ....April 7

Daniel
2:22..April 8
3:25..April 9
3:27..April 10
4:37.. April 11
6:22..April 12
11:32 .... April 13

Hosea
5:15..April 14
6:3.. April 15

Joel
2:1 ....April 16
3:13 .... April 17

Amos
3:7..April 18
8:11..April 19

Micah
6:8..April 20

Malachi
4:2 .... April 21

Matthew

5:7 . . . . April 22
5:8 . . . . April 23
5:13 . . . . April 24
5:39 . . . . April 25
6:6 . . . . April 26
6:28-29 . . . . April 27
6:33 . . . . April 28
6:34 . . . . April 29
7:14 . . . . April 30
8:22 . . . . May 1
9:29 . . . . May 2
10:8 . . . . May 3
10:30 . . . . May 4
11:28-29 . . . . May 5, May 6
12:36 . . . . May 7
12:37 . . . . May 8
13:11-12 . . . . May 9
13:39 . . . . May 10
16:25 . . . . May 11
16:26 . . . . May 12
17:21 . . . . May 13
19:16-17 . . . . May 14
23:11 . . . . May 15
23:25 . . . . May 16
25:29 . . . . May 17

Mark

4:22 . . . . May 18
4:23-24 . . . . May 19
5:18-19 . . . . May 20
6:11 . . . . May 21
6:31 . . . . May 22
8:35 . . . . May 23
8:35-36 . . . . May 24
8:38 . . . . May 25
9:5-6 . . . . May 26
11:24 . . . . May 27
16:15 . . . . May 28
16:20 . . . . May 29, May 30

Luke

1:41 . . . . May 31
1:53 . . . . June 1
1:79 . . . . June 2
4:30 . . . . June 3
5:4 . . . . June 4
6:35-36 . . . . June 5
6:38 . . . . June 6
6:42 . . . . June 7
6:44 . . . . June 8
8:18 . . . . June 9
9:62 . . . . June 10, June 11
10:1 . . . . June 12
10:2 . . . . June 13
10:19 . . . . June 14
10:41-42 . . . . June 15
11:35-36 . . . . June 16
12:32 . . . . June 17, June 18, June 19
12:40 . . . . June 20, June 21
14:33 . . . . June 22
18:17 . . . . June 23
18:22 . . . . June 24
21:36 . . . . June 25
21:37-38 . . . . June 26
22:61-62 . . . . June 27

John

1:1-2 . . . . June 28
1:14 . . . . June 29
4:14 . . . . June 30, July 1, July 2
5:4 . . . . July 3
5:24 . . . . July 4, July 5
6:51 . . . . July 6
9:31 . . . . July 7
10:10 . . . . July 8
13:17 . . . . July 9
14:12 . . . . July 10
14:21 . . . . July 11, July 12
14:23 . . . . July 13
14:27 . . . . July 14, July 15
15:1 . . . . July 16
15:8 . . . . July 17
16:13 . . . . July 18
16:20 . . . . July 19
17:23 . . . . July 20
20:27 . . . . July 21

Acts

1:8 . . . . July 22, July 23
6:4 . . . . July 24
8:5-6 . . . . July 25
8:26 . . . . July 26
9:7 . . . . July 27
9:15 . . . . July 28
26:19 . . . . July 29

Romans

5:3 . . . . July 30
5:5 . . . . July 31, August 1
6:14 . . . . August 2
7:15 . . . . August 3
8:11 . . . . August 4
8:14 . . . . August 5, August 6, August 7
8:26 . . . . August 8
8:27 . . . . August 9
8:28 . . . . August 10
8:37 . . . . August 11, August 12
9:26 . . . . August 13
10:21 . . . . August 14
11:8 . . . . August 15
12:1-2 . . . . August 16, August 17, August 18
12:12 . . . . August 19
14:17-18 . . . . August 20
14:23 . . . . August 21
15:1-2 . . . . August 22
15:3 . . . . August 23
15:13 . . . . August 24

1 Corinthians

1:30-31 . . . . August 25
2:9 . . . . August 26, August 27
2:10-11 . . . . August 28
2:12 . . . . August 29
3:9 . . . . August 30
9:22 . . . . August 31
10:31 . . . . September 1
11:32 . . . . September 2
12:7 . . . . September 3
12:31 . . . . September 4
13:1 . . . . September 5, September 6
13:4-5 . . . . September 7
15:50 . . . . September 8

15:57 . . . . September 9, September 10
16:9 . . . . September 11
16:13 . . . . September 12

2 Corinthians
3:18 . . . . September 13
4:7 . . . . September 14
4:8-9 . . . . September 15
4:17 . . . . September 16, September 17, September 18
6:10 . . . . September 19
6:14 . . . . September 20
6:17 . . . . September 21
7:10 . . . . September 22
12:9 . . . . September 23

Galatians
1:10 . . . . September 24
1:11-12 . . . . September 25
2:20 . . . . September 26, September 27
5:1 . . . . September 28, September 29
5:16 . . . . September 30
5:17 . . . . .October 1
5:22-23 . . . . October 2, October 3, October 4
6:8 . . . . October 5

Ephesians
1:4 . . . . October 6
2:6 . . . . October 7
4:24 . . . . October 8
5:1-2 . . . . October 9
6:10 . . . . October 10
6:12 . . . . October 11, October 12, October 13
6:17 . . . . October 14
6:18 . . . . October 15

Philippians
1:6 . . . . October 16
2:12-13 . . . . October 17, October 18
3:8 . . . . October 19
3:12 . . . . October 20
3:13-14 . . . . October 21
3:14 . . . . October 22
4:6 . . . . .October 23, October 24
4:13 . . . . October 25
4:19 . . . . October 26

Colossians

1:10 . . . . October 27
1:24 . . . . October 28
1:27 . . . . October 29
2:19 . . . . October 30
3:1-2 . . . . October 31
3:15 . . . . November 1
3:16 . . . . November 2
3:17 . . . . November 3
4:6 . . . . November 4

1 Thessalonians

5:18 . . . . November 5, November 6
5:23-24 . . . . November 7

2 Thessalonians

3:3 . . . . November 8

1 Timothy

4:12 . . . . November 9

2 Timothy

1:6 . . . . November 10
1:12 . . . . November 11
1:14 . . . . November 12
2:12 . . . . November 13
2:15 . . . . November 14
2:24 . . . . November 15
4:7 . . . . November 16

Hebrews

3:14 . . . . November 17
4:12 . . . . November 18
4:15 . . . . November 19
11:1 . . . . November 20
11:6 . . . . November 21
12:1 . . . . November 22
12:2 . . . . November 23
13:15 . . . . November 24
13:20-21 . . . . November 25

James

1:4 . . . . November 26
1:5 . . . . November 27

1:12 . . . . .November 28
1:27 . . . . .November 29
4:7 . . . . .November 30
4:7-8 . . . . December 1
4:10 . . . . December 2
5:16 . . . . December 3

1 Peter
1:5 . . . . December 4
1:6 . . . . December 5
1:7 . . . . December 6
1:13 . . . . December 7
4:8 . . . . December 8
4:12 . . . . December 9
4:17 . . . . December 10, December 11
5:6 . . . . December 12
5:6-7 . . . . December 13
5:8 . . . . December 14, December 15
5:10 . . . . December 16

1 John
1:9-10 . . . . December 17
2:17 . . . . December 18, December 19
2:27 . . . . December 20
4:16 . . . . December 21
4:19-20 . . . . December 22

3 John
1:2 . . . . December 23

Jude
1:20-21 . . . . .December 24, December 25

Revelation
1:8 . . . . December 26
12:11 . . . . December 27
14:7 . . . . December 28
19:8 . . . . December 29
19:15 . . . . December 30
21:1 . . . . December 31